Care and Counselling Series

SEXUAL COUNSELLING

BOOKS ON CARE AND COUNSELLING

Library of Pastoral Care

Pastoral Care in Hospitals
NORMAN AUTTON

The Pastor and His Ministry
OWEN BRANDON

In His Own Parish:
Pastoral Care through Parochial Visiting
KENNETH CHILD

Working with Children
ANTHONY DENNEY

Understanding the Adolescent
MICHAEL HARE DUKE

Casework and Pastoral Care
JEAN HEYWOOD

Marriage Counselling
KENNETH PRESTON

Care and Counselling Series

Peace at the Last
NORMAN AUTTON

Principles of Pastoral Counselling
R. S. LEE

You Alone Care
HEATHER MCKENZIE

Una Kroll

SEXUAL COUNSELLING

LONDON
SPCK

First published 1980
SPCK
Holy Trinity Church
Marylebone Road
London NW1 4DU

Filmset in Great Britain by
Northumberland Press Ltd,
Gateshead, Tyne and Wear
and printed by
Fletcher and Son Ltd
Norwich

ISBN 0 281 03752 3

*For my clients
friends and colleagues
who have taught me
to rejoice in the gift
of sexuality*

Contents

Acknowledgements

I am grateful to many of my clients, friends and colleagues who shared their insights into human sexuality and its problems with me, so enabling me to deepen my own understanding of the work of sexual counsellors.

I thank my publishers and Miss Gillian Hanscombe for reading early typescripts and making valuable criticisms which helped me to prepare this final text. The responsibility for the completed work and for any opinions, theories or conclusions expressed therein is mine alone.

The extracts by Fr Adrian Hastings and Daphne Nash from *New Blackfriars* are used with the editor's permission. The poem 'The Thing called Love' is quoted with the author's permission.

Introduction

Good counsellors lack no clients
(W. Shakespeare: *Measure for Measure*)

Thousands of books have been written about sex, sexual identity, sexual behaviour, sexual problems and sexual therapy. This one also considers these topics, but it differs from many other books in that it describes the tensions experienced by many Christian clients and counsellors when they encounter practical problems over sexual matters either in their own lives or in their relations with other people. Some of these tensions are recognizable in the story of Rita who came to me with a personal problem.

Rita came into my room one day and burst into tears almost as soon as she sat down.

'I don't know what to do,' she sobbed, 'George has left me. Well, he hasn't actually gone yet, but he says he won't go on living with me and the children unless I agree to take his girl friend into our home. He says everybody's doing it. Are they?'

She turned her desperate eyes towards me, looking for some signs of hope in my response. 'What am I to do?' she went on without waiting for an answer, 'I took it for granted that our marriage would last. I didn't think this kind of thing could happen to people like us!' Her words tumbled out in a jerky way. 'I don't believe in divorce. I didn't think George did either. I can't leave him. I've nowhere to go. The children adore him. They'll be heart-broken if he leaves. Surely he can't really expect me to put up with his mistress living with us? Oh God, what a mess it is.' Her voice trailed off into a squeaky sob.

I sighed because I knew that she and George were faced with a long period of suffering, tension and indecision. They would probably torment themselves during the process of trying to find out exactly what had gone wrong with their marriage. They might change their minds many times before they could settle on a permanent decision about their future. In the long run they

I

might part and go their separate ways. Possibly, if they were both willing to work hard at mending their relationship or forging a new one, they could decide to stay together. In time George's love for another woman might become a memory from the past. Alternatively, they might try to take his Sarah into their home, and they might even make a success of the experiment. At this stage of their problem it was impossible to predict what would happen.

'It's all my fault,' Rita said. 'I know it is. My mother always said that a good wife should be able to hold on to her husband if she looked after his needs, kept him happy and gave him children.' She looked even more miserable than before.

'What's happening to the children?' I asked, trying to take her mind off her imagined or real inadequacies, which were confirming her sense of guilt and failure.

'Oh, they still seem quite happy,' she said. 'They don't know anything about it yet. Oh God, how am I going to tell them? And what's to become of us? We were so happy only a few weeks ago.'

Rita's world had collapsed. The next few months proved to be worse than either of us had anticipated. Rita felt so guilty about her feelings of jealousy that she tried to overcome them by agreeing to try George's plan. Sarah came to live with them, but after a while they all realized that the experiment was a failure from everyone's point of view, especially the children's. Instead they tried to reach a working compromise. George began to spend three nights a week with Rita and the children. He spent the rest of the week with Sarah. When Sarah became pregnant, however, he left his marital home altogether.

Rita's children reacted to their parents' unhappiness. Their house was no longer the secure and loving place they had known during their early years of life. John, the elder of the two, became very quiet and withdrawn. His teachers complained that his school work no longer measured up to his potential ability. He scarcely ever brought friends home. Tina, who was two years younger than John, and had been only nine years old when her mother and father had finally split, became impossible to manage. She was noisy and rude at home, and she gave her teachers a hard time at school as she never seemed to want to learn anything at all. She spent most of her time in lessons trying to get some of the other children in her class to behave as badly as she did herself. Tina obviously blamed her mother for her father's

2

departure. Whenever there were rows over her untidiness, poor school reports and petty thefts, she would fling back her own angry accusations at her mother, who was often reduced to tears by her daughter's cruel words. By the time she was thirteen years old Tina was a very unpleasant person to live with except when her father took her out to visit his new family. She adored her half-brother and flaunted her love for him when she came home to Rita and John. There was so much bad feeling between them all over this that Rita suggested that Tina should go and live with her father. Sarah, however, would not hear of such an arrangement and so the unhappy tensions at home continued.

Rita found it very difficult to give George the divorce he wanted. She still loved her husband and although she saw very little of him once he had another family to support, she went on hoping that he would return to her one day. She was horrified when her solicitor told her that George might be able to get a legal divorce against her wishes after five years of separation from her. In the end, rather than face that humiliation, she gave George what he so passionately wanted.

After the divorce Rita remained profoundly unhappy. She was convinced that she could never again form a relationship which might lead to her own remarriage. She continued to visit me in the years following her final separation from George. On her regular monthly visits for her supplies of the drugs which controlled her depression and made her life bearable she nearly always brought up the subject of her future plans.

'I just don't know what to do,' she would say in a plaintive voice which echoed that of her first visit. 'I'm growing into a sexually frustrated old bitch. I get so tense wanting George, but I don't feel free to find anyone else. The psychiatrist you sent me to see said that it was absurd to consider myself still married to George when our relationship is so obviously dead. He said that I had every right to find someone else and seize another chance of happiness. He even told me he was sure that God wouldn't mind. But the vicar didn't seem so sure. He said he wouldn't blame me if I did try to find success with another man. But when I asked him if I could be married in church he told me that it wouldn't be possible unless George died first, although he did promise that he would give us a blessing in church after a registry office wedding. That sounds to me like a second-class event. Why should George have to die before I could have a proper wedding service? Oh doctor, it's all such a muddle,' she

3

would say, and often the tears would begin to flow again. 'I never thought our marriage would turn out the way it did. George and I were married in church. We were both believing Christians and we promised to stay with each other for the rest of our lives. We meant it, too. It wasn't just me. George wanted to make those vows as much as I did. His faith seemed so strong. Why, up to the day we parted we always went to church together for Sunday worship. The whole family did. I often thought that old saying about "the family that prays together, stays together", must be true for us. Where did we go wrong? What happened to George's beliefs? What's going to happen to mine in the future? No two people give me the same advice. I feel torn between the vicar, who seems to imply that I should be able to be faithful to my original marriage vows while George is alive, and the psychiatrist who sees no reason for me to turn my back on my deepest need to be loved. The one reinforces my belief about what I ought to do. The other urges me to do what I really want to do. Each of them seems to think that his point of view is the right one. I wish I knew what God means me to do.'

Rita's story must remain unfinished. Although I have altered the details in order to protect everyone's privacy the story is true in its essentials and illustrates the kind of practical problem which often brings people to a doctor or counsellor for help. Rita is still alive and so there is hope that she will eventually be able to resolve the spiritual, psychological and bodily tensions which are still causing her so much distress. Her case history leaves many questions unanswered. I am aware that I have told the story only from her point of view. I do not know what has happened to George and his new family. The children have moved away and I cannot tell whether or not their own childhood experiences will affect their ability to make satisfactory personal relationships. Since I know both the vicar and the psychiatrist to whom Rita turned in her trouble I believe that I can understand both their points of view and I can see how each reinforced certain attitudes which were already present in Rita and caused her to feel torn apart.

4

This book is about people like Rita. It is about sex—a fact of life with which women and men have had to contend ever since they became self-aware and capable of choice. It is also about some of the ideas current in contemporary western society about sex, sexuality, sexual behaviour and the many problems which occur simply because human beings are sexual persons. Some of these ideas come to us from the past. Others emerge from scientific discovery and new insights born out of experience. Sometimes these ideas bring people into direct conflict of opinion, as, for instance, Rita found out when she went to two different advisers who held opposing views on the rightness of the remarriage of divorcees during a former partner's lifetime.

I am particularly interested in these conflicting ideas about sex and sexual conduct since they cause tensions in the lives of so many people who are wrestling with sexual problems. It is my belief that many people's sexual problems cannot be satisfactorily solved until their underlying attitudes towards their difficulties can be examined and understood in the light of their historical antecedents and their contemporary values. Many of these underlying attitudes are grounded in people's individual and corporate religious and moral beliefs about sex, sexuality and sexual conduct. I believe that it is in this area that modern Christians can make a relevant contribution to contemporary thinking and practice.

In most western countries today the laws, customs and cultural life of the whole community are still affected by the strong links between Church and State which existed in an earlier period of history. The gradual decline of Christian influence on society in general has meant that many other influences and unofficial opinions which have always co-existed with and often been opposed to official Church doctrine have been able to make a powerful impact on people's attitudes towards sex and its related issues. These other strands of thought which are particularly

5

strong in contemporary western society have forced many people, including Christians, to rethink and revaluate their own attitudes towards human sexuality, its nature, purposes and problems.

Christians are no more immune from conflict than anyone else in society. Within their own community Christians often disagree with one another on important matters. Their current conflicting opinions about issues relating to sex, gender, orientation, sexual conduct and sex-related issues like the roles of women and men in society, the acceptance of practising homosexuals into the priesthood, the remarriage of divorcees in church, the toleration of contraception, abortion and sterilization in the community, are important in their own right but they also point to even more fundamental disagreements about the nature of humankind and of God. It seems to me to be important that some of these conflicting views about human nature and God should be allowed to surface at the very outset of this book since they inevitably affect the way different individuals and groups of Christians will approach the practical sexual problems with which they have to wrestle from time to time.

One of the most important areas of fundamental conflict between Christians relates to their views on bodily existence, the relation of soul and body, of spirit and matter to each other. Christian attitudes towards sex have never been uniform because Christians have never been able to agree whole-heartedly with one another about their attitudes towards the fact of bodily existence. Some of their most important differences of opinion originate in the history of the early Christian Church.

Rooted as they were in Judaism, which itself was affected by many other religious influences, the earliest Christians formed themselves into groups and developed into communities at a time in history and in regions of the world where the influence of dualistic philosophies, with their tendencies to see soul and body, spirit and matter as separate entities in antithesis to each other, was particularly strong.[1] It is true that the impact of the person of Christ on his immediate Jewish disciples was so powerful, and his teachings, with their emphasis on love as the fundamental law of relationship with God and one's neighbour, were so arresting that the very first Christians probably had little reason to argue about the doctrinal aspects of their religious beliefs about the body, but when the Gospel took root in the gentile communities the leaders of the young Christian Church found themselves trying to explain the Gospel to two sets of people who came to Christianity from different traditions. At first all Christians were probably agreed that the human body could be used as a vehicle of love and was so used as an instrument of divine love when Christ put on human flesh. As time passed, however, and the discussions about the nature of Christ got under way, so the arguments about the nature of humankind also developed. These debates were influenced by the scriptural references to the origins of women and men, and the allusions to their fallen nature in the Genesis narratives, and by gnostic strands of thought which were current during the formative years of institutional Christianity.[2] The arguments raged during the first four centuries after Christ's death and resurrection, but the formal ending of the debate in the formulation of the doctrinal creeds which are part of our received tradition did not end the discussions. These continue today.

Although some Christians have always regarded the human body as inherently good and have seen sex as a God-given gift through which human beings can express their love for God and each other, others have apparently regarded the living body as a necessary home for the soul during a person's lifetime. Unlike the people in the first group, who have generally treated body and soul as a unity, they have thought of body and soul as separate entities, often set against each other. In the past many people in this latter group have also thought of sex as a consequence

7

of the Fall. Those who have seen sex in this way have usually been more suspicious of the body than those who have not thought it right to make a direct link between original sin and sex. Historically the opinions of those who have distrusted the body and its sexual functions have prevailed with most Christians over many generations. These views led many people to believe that the body was inferior to the soul, as matter was thought to be inferior to spirit.

Although such opinions did not tie in well with fully developed incarnational theology they nevertheless gained popular support and they had a profound effect both on Christian attitudes towards the roles of women and men in the community and on moral law. The body became linked in many people's minds with nature, the earth, the sinful desires of human beings and especially with women who were sexual beings, temptresses and child-bearers. The spirit became identified with God, with heaven, with self-control over bodily urges, with human rationality. Since the body was thought of as inferior to the spiritual soul, and bodily functions as less holy than spiritual activities, there was a proper logic in the widely accepted view that marriage was a lower state of life than celibacy. People who thought of sex in connection with their fallen human nature could view marriage with favour only because it was plainly God's will that human beings should continue to be the stewards of God's creation. People who did not marry were expected to discipline themselves by abstaining from overt sexual activity. In recent times the alternative view which sees body and soul as a unity, and which also sees Christ as a sexual person has begun to be much more popular than it used to be. This view finds its justification in incarnational theology.[3]

People who hold to the view that body and soul, matter and spirit are a unity and who rejoice in Christ's redeeming work can see God as much at work in the body as in the soul. Since they do not see life in terms of opposites in separation but consider everything as part of a whole they are more able to think of men and women as members of God's family whose differences enhance their unitedness and emphasize their equal dignity in the sight of God. They are inclined to rejoice in the body as much as in the spirit and to see matter and spirit as interchangeable forms of energy whose origins are in God. Since they believe the body to be as holy as spirit they make no distinction between marriage and celibacy and are usually able to see sexual activity as good in itself apart from its obvious biological purpose, although they are well aware that many people misuse themselves in ways which alienate them from God and one another.

All Christians, whether they distrust the body or rejoice in its potential, whether they see body and soul in separation or in unity, whether or not they believe that original sin and sex are directly linked, find their inspiration and hope for humankind in the person of Christ and his teaching about the primacy of love in relationship. As Love redeemed humankind, so it is the primacy of love which rescues sex from being used in selfish and sinful ways. In order to emphasize the relationship between love and personhood as exemplified in Christ and proclaimed in the Gospel, Christians have tried to put their beliefs into practice. In relation to sex they have tried to give those beliefs expression by drawing up laws and codes of behaviour which seek to preserve the fundamental principle that love and sex must go hand in hand if human beings are to be faithful stewards of God's gifts. Some of these laws, like the ones on adultery, were taken over from religions and philosophies which were more ancient than Christianity. Others, like the canons insisting on celibacy for priests of the Roman communion, developed because of particular circumstances. Some, like the laws prohibiting the remarriage of divorcees during the lifetime of a former partner, developed as the Church grew in size and influence. From the time of Constantine many Christian laws and codes of practice were taken over by the State and imposed on all individuals in the whole community whether or not they were Christians.

In western society the gradual separation of Church and State has meant that many of the laws and customs which regulate sexual behaviour do not now apply with equal vigour in Church and State. Some Christians regret the loss of Christian influence which has followed the secularization of society. Others see the current turmoil over sex and its related problems as an opportunity to revaluate their own attitudes and discover new insights about sexuality compatible with their belief in the primacy of love in all relationships. Many of these Christians who have struggled to understand human sexuality more fully are now able to think positively about the unity of body and soul, spirit and matter. This fundamental shift in their thinking has also enabled them to take a fresh look at some of the ways in which they approach sexual problems and the people who are distressed by them.

I am one of these Christians. I was once infected with a dualism of which I was largely unconscious and discovered it only when I was drawn into sexual counselling as part of my ordinary work as a family doctor, I found myself then struggling to help clients, many of whom were also Christians, to find solutions to their sexual problems compatible with their faith and mine. A fuller understanding of incarnational theology, which is the best remedy for dualism, has certainly helped me and many of my clients to rejoice in our bodily existence and to take a new look at the ways in which we seek to be whole people.

This book is an account of our combined efforts to understand human sexuality both in the light of some of the more recent scientific discoveries about the nature of sex, and of the insights drawn from incarnational theology. It also records a number of our attempts to look at some of the religious questions lying behind many of the sexual problems which people bring to counsellors.

This work is not an advanced textbook. It is a primer written by a counsellor who has also been a client and who, therefore, writes with both sides in mind. It concentrates on those sexual problems which are frequently presented to non-specialist counsellors, but it also includes some unusual problems with special significance for people's understanding of human sexuality. It focuses on the people who have the problems more than on the problems themselves and tries to pay particular attention to the nature of the relationships between clients and counsellors.

In writing this book I have profited greatly from the knowledge and experience of many clients, friends and counsellors whose accumulated wisdom has often enlightened me when my own knowledge and skill has faltered. Their experience has been included in the case studies which describe real situations although the identities of my clients and professional colleagues have been disguised in order to protect their privacy. These case histories also reflect the fact that I am a European doctor and the clients who come to me for sexual counselling are predominantly Caucasians, even though I practise in a multi-racial urban community near London. They also reflect the fact that more heterosexuals than homosexuals come to me with sexual problems, although my records show that as many homosexuals as heterosexuals ask for counselling for psychosexual problems.

ONE
Sex and Self

Most men and women can accept themselves as they are without difficulty. They are confident about their sexual identity because when they were born their parents felt certain about their anatomical sex. They grew up with the expectation that they would have distinctive biological roles in adult life, and they enjoy being women and men throughout their lives.

Some people, however, do not have such happy experiences. At some stage of their lives they encounter a problem which makes them feel insecure about their sexual identity. A number of these people come to sexual counsellors for help. Their problems raise questions about social 'norms' and expectations as the following case history shows.

Jeremy and Lucy were a happily married couple. Both of them had good jobs and between them they earned enough money to pay the mortgage on their home.

After the first five years of their marriage they decided that they had sufficient financial reserves to be able to start a family, but to their dismay Lucy did not become pregnant. A year later they went to their family doctor and asked for further investigations.

The doctor referred them to an excellent sub-fertility unit, and after some routine tests had been carried out Jeremy and Lucy were each given a buccal-smear sex test. To the family doctor's surprise he subsequently received a letter from the hospital telling him that Jeremy's sex test indicated that he was a genetic female and, therefore, sterile. Although Lucy had female genes she suffered from an unusual condition which made it very unlikely that she could ever bear children.

The doctor told the couple that they were infertile but he did not confront them with the startling news that they shared the same genetic sex. Moreover, he had never suspected this to be the case despite his having known the couple for some time, having taken their sexual history and having examined them physically. Jeremy had rather small genitalia and scanty facial and pubic hair, and Lucy complained of very infrequent, scanty, menstrual periods. The doctor had, however, seen fertile men and women with similar physical characteristics before, and so he had overlooked the finer details of their history which might have prompted him to entertain the same suspicions that had crossed the specialist's mind when he had ordered the buccal-smear tests.

It is probable that the doctor's decision to tell the couple the truth, but not the whole truth, was a wise one, for the psychological effect on Jeremy of discovering that he was genetically female might have been disastrous. As it was, he continued to think of himself as a man and he was able to continue enjoying adequate sexual relations with his wife. Jeremy and Lucy were able to adapt to their infertility and they eventually decided not to adopt any children but to accept their childless state.

This couple were highly unusual, of course. They both suffered from rare conditions and their coming together in marriage must have made them an almost unique partnership. However, their story illustrates how difficult it can be to decide who is a woman and who a man. Modern doctors are far less confident than their predecessors used to be about assigning babies, young people and adults to one or the other sex on anatomical appearances alone. In addition to this, scientists are not yet sure that they know exactly how sex and personality characteristics are linked. Their theories sometimes contradict one another. They also disagree as to whether people's sexual orientation is determined by genetic or environmental factors, or both.

Although it is still impossible to make definitive statements about any of these matters it is useful to look at some of the recent thinking about the factors which contribute to human beings' self-confidence in their sexual identity.

Sex and the genes

It used to be taken for granted that the human race was divided into women and men and that the external appearance of a new-born baby could be used to determine its sex.

Anatomical sex is generally a good guide to genetic sex, but throughout human history babies have been born whose anatomical sex was obviously indeterminate, and some of these still grow up in the wrong sex.

Until the twentieth century most of the children whose sex was uncertain at birth were arbitrarily allocated to one sex in the hope that the right one had been chosen, and in the expectation that cultural conditioning would enable the child to conform to her or his assigned role. It is now possible to determine the genetic sex of such a child. Using that knowledge, together with a detailed knowledge of the anatomical appearance of the child, its existent organs and its blood endocrine levels, it is possible to make an accurate assessment of the potential of the child to grow into a woman or a man, even though it is known that the adult is likely to be infertile. In the past some of these children, like Jeremy, grew up without realizing that there was anything wrong with them. Now, once the best choice of sex has been made, other decisions follow. The child has to be examined regularly as it grows up in case plastic surgery or supplementary hormone therapy becomes necessary. Occasionally, as the child develops, it becomes apparent that the original choice will have to be changed because the child is obviously happier in the sex opposite to that chosen in infancy. A great deal can be done, and is being done, to help these people to feel secure in their sexual identity so that they can take on the sexual roles which either were chosen for them in infancy, or which they themselves have chosen at a later date.

People who do not possess an average anatomy or whose physical appearance does not correspond with their genetic

14

sex challenge all the old assumptions about men and women being distinguishable from each other by measurable anatomical and physiological characteristics. Their existence also makes it difficult to formulate precise definitions about femaleness and maleness which can indicate exactly what it means to be a man or a woman. Since, however, the majority of men and women are easy to separate anatomically and genetically, the exceptions are often thought to uphold the norms. The idea that exceptions prove the rule might have been credible a hundred years ago when relatively little was known about the development of the human personality. In recent years, however, the old assumptions about sexual identity's close link with genetic sex and anatomical sex have been challenged by the arrival of the new concept of gender identity.

Sex and gender

Within the last two decades a number of people who are transexuals have spoken openly and perceptively about their sex-role confusions, and by doing so they have helped scientists to think more precisely about individuals whose anatomy and genes correspond to one sex but whose perception of themselves convinces them that they belong to the opposite one.

Transexuals like Jan Morris in England and Dr Renée Richards in America have openly testified to the fact that, although they had lived as men and had fathered children, they felt that they were really women living in the wrong body. Their condition has been described as a confusion of gender identity. Gender is a relatively new concept which describes how people relate to themselves as women or men. When people think about their gender they have to rely on their own understanding of what it means to be a woman or a man, and they use that yardstick when they are trying to decide who they are.

Jan Morris has described how she felt when she was

three or four years old and realized that she had been born into the wrong body, a male body:

My conviction of mistaken sex was still no more than a blur, tucked away at the back of my mind, but if I was not unhappy, I was habitually puzzled. Even then, that silent fresh childhood above the sea seemed to me strangely incomplete. I felt a yearning for I know not what, as though there were a piece missing from my pattern, or some element in me that should be hard and permanent, but was instead soluble and diffuse.[1]

Jan Morris, Renée Richards and many other transexuals have felt so strongly about their plight that they have persuaded doctors, psychiatrists and surgeons to help them to change their sex. Their gender identity has been more important to them than their genetic or anatomical sex, even when those last two aspects of themselves were acting in harmony with each other. They have been willing to undergo long periods of time receiving hormone therapy to feminize them. They have dressed and 'passed' as women for some time before undergoing corrective surgery to acquire a female appearance and be able to have sexual intercourse as women.

Sex-change operations have been well publicized in western society. Records show that the majority of these operations are carried out on men who want to become as much like women as possible because they are convinced that they are really women who have been born into the wrong body. Relatively few women ask for plastic surgery in order to live as men, but a number of them do take male hormones and are able to adopt a male life style.

Much work remains to be done by and with the co-operation of transexuals before the full implications of their existence can be worked out. Theirs is a comparatively rare problem which deserves public sympathy and understanding rather than the voyeurism they sometimes attract.

Gender confusion is not confined to transexuals. Any physical feature which contradicts people's ideas of what

16

it means to be women and men can provoke a sex-role confusion. This is often found for instance when members of one sex exhibit certain physical characteristics which they consider to be proper only to the opposite sex. Many women, for instance, feel very shy because they are hirsute. Men may feel equally shy if they are not well covered with body hair. Some women mind being flat chested because they can feel secure about their gender identity only if they have well-developed breasts. Similarily, many men feel somewhat inadequate unless they have large genitals. As far as they are concerned, their gender identity is closely linked to their bodily appearance which, to their way of thinking, must agree with their expectation of normality and compare well with the anatomy of other people of the same sex.

It is not only anatomical features which matter to people. Sexual function is of prime importance to most women and men. Most young women look expectantly for signs of their menarche and feel themselves to be fully developed only when they see regular and adequate menstrual periods. Young men may feel shy when their voices break, but they generally feel reassured when they experience sexual erections and realize that their night-dreams and nocturnal emissions are a sign of adult manhood. For this reason all adolescent problems over sexual function merit serious and sympathetic treatment. Counsellors have an important educational role to play for their adolescent clients who are troubled by anatomical and physiological deficiencies of any kind.

Women and men who suffer from more severe feelings of gender inferiority which do not yield to simple information and counselling may not want to change their sex like some transexuals, but their reactions to their problems can be very similar to those of transexuals. Women will, for instance, sometimes go to great lengths and considerable expense to banish unwanted hair. Some of them will insist on having breast implants. Many men try to develop their muscles and grow more hair, and some worry a great deal about the size of their genitalia.

People who feel insecure about their gender identity can often be reassured if their organs continue to function properly. Although she will continue to feel sensitive about her facial hair, a woman will usually feel more secure in her identity if she has managed to bear a child in spite of her hairiness. The young man who has fathered a child will often feel less worried about the size of his penis than he did before he knew himself to be fertile.

In order to feel comfortable and at home with themselves most men and women need to feel secure in their sexual identity if they are to feel themselves to be worthy of the love and affection of other people. While it is enough for some people to be able to measure up to their own ideas of normality it seems that many people can feel secure only if they also conform to other people's standards of normality. This desire to feel secure in themselves and acceptable to others leads many people to alter their appearance and behaviour so that they look and act more like the kind of man or woman they want to become. It is not enough for them to have the right genes and anatomical organs which function properly. They cannot rely on their feelings about their gender. Real security for these people means that they must also behave in ways that are appropriate to their sex. Their character is affected by their sexual identity.

Character formation begins at a very early age. It is affected by parental, social, cultural and religious influences, and these influences often persist into adult life. Some people never move away from the ideas acquired in their youth as to what being a woman or man really entails. Others discover that they cannot cling to these youthful ideas. The reality of their own personalities challenges them to change their ideas about how sex and character are linked.

Sex and character

Among adults living in western societies there continues to be a widespread belief that manly men are ambitious, highly sexed, dominant and aggressive individuals and that womanly women are retiring, pure, receptive and gentle human beings. The character qualities of ambitiousness, sexiness, dominance and aggressiveness are thus linked with maleness and acquire a 'masculine' label, while reticence, purity, receptiveness and gentleness become 'feminine' virtues. A man who fails to behave in a masculine way risks being thought of as an inadequate male, a 'girlish' boy, a 'sissy' or a *'femme'*. A woman who offends against the conventions expected from one of her sex may expect to be accused of being a 'mannish' woman, a 'butch' person or a freak.

This tendency to link particular personality traits with people's sex has induced millions of mothers and fathers to teach their children to modify their behaviour in order to conform to well-defined, stereotyped, sex-linked roles so that when they grow up the children will be confident in their roles as men or women. The belief that certain character traits are inherently sex linked can make children and adults try to live up to their stereotypes even if this means their behaving in ways which do not reflect their deepest feelings about themselves.

Western society is still heavily influenced by the notion that it is natural for men and women to adopt special roles according to their sex. Girls and boys are taught about these roles. They are treated in special and different ways which are thought appropriate to their sex. They are gradually conditioned to have different expectations of life when they become sexually mature. This social conditioning is reinforced by the still prevalent and popular psycho-analytic theories about the role of sex and sexuality in the development of the human psyche.

When the nineteenth-century analysts were formulating

their theories about the role of sex in character formation they were looking for explanations for the psychological disturbances which they had observed in their adult patients. Freud and Jung, in particular, tended to regard their clients' behaviour, fantasies and neurotic traits as being intimately related to sex and subconscious sexual experiences. Their analytical theories have been influential in psychological medicine and have become widely known outside that discipline. Although many of Freud's and Jung's theories were challenged and modified by later analysts, they are still acceptable to a large number of people and are still widely taught to those engaged in psychotherapy or pastoral counselling.

The influence of Freud and Jung is particularly strong in the western hemisphere and the result has been that many pastoral counsellors trained in the west have absorbed and been partially conditioned by analytic ideas which they have picked up during their training. During their working lives counsellors will meet many clients who also have some knowledge of analytic theories although the original ideas may have been distorted during the process of transmission from person to person. Considerable problems of communication may occur between counsellors and clients when, for instance, Freud's oedipal complex and his theories about 'penis envy' jostle uneasily alongside Jung's ideas about 'animus' and 'anima' in the minds of both counsellors and clients. Moreover, since present-day people are very familiar with these analytic concepts their critical faculties are often suspended. Some of them believe Freudian and Jungian theories to be true without even questioning them.

This tendency to swallow Freudian or Jungian ideas uncritically can often be observed during discussions on the role of sex in character formation. It is quite common to hear someone either on the platform or in the audience say that everyone knows that men's bodies contain vestigial elements of female organs while women's bodies house rudimentary male sex organs and that because of this there must be corresponding psychological entities within everyone's personality. The people who make this kind of statement evidently do not realize that they might be *non-sequiturs*, even though many of them can accept the idea that a person's gender does not necessarily depend upon his or her genetic or anatomical sex.

Somewhat similar statements about the link between anatomy and personality are sometimes made by people who have thought critically about the subject and still believe that the sexual organs express themselves through the psyche. This point of view is well put by an eminent post-Freudian analyst, Erik Erickson. He suggests that the nature of the male and female sexual organs leads to men and women behaving differently from each other. According to him the thrusting, active penis is reflected in the active and dynamic pragmatic approach of the typical male, whereas the inner space of the woman, her receptive womb, finds expression in her gentle, peaceful, rather static orientation.[2] Erickson and his followers seem to have forgotten that the womb can be a powerful expelling organ as well as a passive hollow one, and that the penis can be flaccid as well as erect, yet their ideas about male dynamism and female passivity persist because they confirm already existing and ingrained social attitudes about the proper functions of men and women in relation to each other in society.

These kinds of definitive statement about the links between anatomy and psychology are based upon Freud's early theories about sex-linked character traits and Jung's concepts about the presence of 'anima' at subconscious levels of men's personalities and 'animus' within women's psyches. It is often forgotten, however, that when Freud and Jung did their early research they were heavily influenced by the patriarchial society in which they had grown up. Even during his own lifetime Freud modified some of his early views. One of his successors, Dr Robert Seidenberg, has written:

In 1932 Freud recanted and advised against equating any particular psychological trait or characteristic with either masculinity or femininity, even such opposites as activity or passivity which had been solidly esconced in all psychoanalysis as male 'nature' and female 'nature' respectively.[3]

Unfortunately Freud's later work is less well remembered on the whole than his earliest utterances which made such a powerful impact on society when they were openly discussed for the first time.

Jung's views are even more firmly entrenched in many people's minds than Freud's, and his ideas about complexes and about the unconscious 'shadow side' of the human personality may be said to have passed into the collective unconscious of western society, so powerful an influence do they exert over the minds of so many people who have had no formal training in Freudian or Jungian theory. The whole concept of 'animus' and 'anima' depends upon there being identifiable differences between men's and women's personality traits, so that elements of the former can be detected within the latter and vice versa.

These analytic theories are important and must be considered carefully, but they are so familiar and well documented that they need no further expansion here. (*See* Selected Bibliography.)

Other less well-known research work done since Freud, Jung and their immediate associates and pupils were alive, suggests that it is not nearly so easy to distinguish between the sexes on the basis of distinctive sex-linked personality traits as we originally thought. Currently, even the correlation between male hormones and aggression, which has been taken for granted for many years, is suspect. Research studies during the past twenty years have suggested that:

Women are at least as aggressive as men, but society forces them to control or channel this aggression, and the consequence of this is an increase in apprehension or anxiety concerning aggression.[4]

After a comprehensive review of all the literature on this subject, another scientist, Lesley Rogers, concludes:

On available evidence the differing concentrations of androgens in males and females cannot explain human sex differences in sexual and aggressive behaviour or on psychophysical and cognitive tasks. It has been impossible to control [the experiments] for cultural factors.[5]

She warns her readers against drawing any premature conclusions:

Premature extrapolation should be strenuously avoided; it is all too prevalent in this field. Experiments on men are difficult, if not impossible to do; yet, if our rush to explain Man leads us to dangerously wrong conclusions we may wind up retarding our search rather than assisting it.[6]

The same necessary caution must be extended towards evaluating the observed differences in the behaviour of men and women where non-hormonal influences may be at work. In a major study for the Department of Employment in Great Britain, published in 1974, Dr J. S. King, a psychologist, writes about the selection of men and women for particular jobs. He comments:

We have contended that the development of these sex-stereotypes reflects sex-role learning rather than any intrinsic differences between the sexes. Interviewers should be aware of the large overlap between the sexes on most aspects of human behaviour, and of the smallness of the differences between the sexes when set against the huge amount of variation within the sexes. They should also be aware that their judgement may be influenced, to a certain extent, by the sex role adjustment of the applicants.[7]

The arguments about the degree to which genetic biological factors and social environmental influences contribute to the differences which distinguish the behaviour

23

of men and women from each other are not yet over. The evidence on either side remains inconclusive and there is need for more interdisciplinary research in this field. One very interesting new approach has been described by Dr Ullian, who suggests that people's concepts about gender alter at different stages of their personal development. In a paper called 'The Development of Conceptions of Masculinity and Femininity' she says:

The model to be presented does not view the development of male and female personalities as a function of biology, nor as a function of social conditioning. Rather, it suggests that both biological and societal factors may be differentially important at various levels of development. It is postulated that with increasing age, there are shifts in the kinds of interpretation the individual gives to biological and social differences *per se*, which shed light on the psychological aspects of masculinity and femininity.[8]

Dr Ullian also thinks that children pass through six different levels or phases as they grow to maturity, and her observations indicate a pattern in children's and young adults' behaviour of alternating acceptance and rejection of sex-role norms. Her studies have led her to believe that:

Despite the child's growing awareness of the arbitrary or socially determined nature of male and female differences, there are significant developmental shifts in the way that information is used to make judgements about the need or desirability to conform to stereotypes of masculinity and femininity.[9]

Finally she thinks that:

The end point of sex-role development proceeds beyond the mere acceptance of conventional notions of masculinity and femininity.[10]

If Ullian is right this means that people can expect to change their ideas about how much their behaviour should conform to social expectations which are based on sexual stereotypes, so that when they are mature they are no longer chained by their fears of flaunting social convention and are free to behave in ways which accord with their own evaluation of their authentic selves.

There can be no doubt about the importance of the links between sex and character even though the exact way in which those links operate must remain speculative. Men and women who feel confident about their sexuality and who feel in harmony with their chosen social role are able to relate to other people with interest and ease so that they can form overt sexual relationships with others on a self-assured basis. Those, on the other hand, who are confused about their true sex, gender or social role often find it difficult to make satisfying personal relationships with other people.

Personal relationships depend not only upon people's biological sex, their gender and established social roles but also upon their sexual orientation which determines the kind of people by whom they are sexually aroused.

Sexual orientation and sexual arousal

Orientation

It is common to hear people describe themselves as hetero-phile or homophile, heterosexual or homosexual, 'straight' or 'gay', as if all human beings could be neatly divided into those who are capable of loving people of the opposite sex or those who are attracted to people of the same sex; but statistics reveal a more subtle pattern. They show that in western society a relatively large proportion of the population is exclusively homosexual in orientation, (variously estimated as 5%–15%). A similar number of people are bisexual in nature, being able to relate sexually either to members of the opposite sex or to those of their own sex. A very small number of people are sexually aroused only by children. It is also well known that sexual orientation varies during one person's life experience, since all human beings pass through various phases during their sexual development. Very young children, for instance, are primarily interested only in their own bodies. Older pre-pubescent children pass through a latent sexual phase. In early adolescence many of them can be sexually aroused by young people of their own sex even though they may have no genital contact. In late adolescence most young adults become heterosexuals but others mature as homo-sexuals. In this context there is no intention of equating adolescence with the teenage years of people's lives, nor is it suggested that homosexuals are 'fixated' adolescents.

There are a number of theories about how men and women develop their sexual orientation. Genes, hormones and cultural factors have all been thought to be prime determinants of sexual predilection and the capacity of one individual to be sexually aroused by several different people. Experiments to analyse the precise parts played by genetic, hormonal and environmental factors in the deve-lopment of sexual excitability are notoriously difficult to devise. Most of the laboratory work in this field has been done with animals, and, as it is known that the hormonal constitution of each species varies, this fact has to be care-fully considered when attempting to extrapolate methods and theories which are appropriate for one species to another. The results of laboratory experiments on animals and human beings are often interpreted differently by different observers. Sometimes opinions are even marshal-led as facts to underpin a person's particular point of view.

A great deal of controversy still exists, for instance, about the normality or abnormality of homosexuality in relation to heterosexuality, and this is one of the areas of controversy where opinion tends to get cited as fact. Heterosexuals who make up the majority of the world's population are commonly thought of as normal by virtue of their numbers and their evident importance in the physical reproduction of the human species. Consequently homosexuals and bisexuals are very often seen as perverts, deviants, abnormal human beings or cases of arrested devlopment, especially if they allow themselves any overt expression of their sexuality. Any serious student who reads the literature on this subject will find plenty of challenges to this view that only one form of sexuality is normal and every variant is abnormal. At the same time many students of the subject recognize that conclusive evidence is not yet forthcoming to support any statement about the genesis of heterosexuality or any other variants of sexuality which could be applied universally to all people and command the acceptance of everyone. Sexual arousal does not only depend on people's sexual orientation. There are other factors which contribute to their ability to respond to sexual stimuli. After all heterosexual men do not fall in love with all women but only with some, and lesbian women do not want to have sexual intercourse with every woman they meet but only with some of those who arouse them sexually.

Sexual arousal
It is known that people respond sexually to stimuli which enter their awareness through any of the senses. Sight, smell, hearing, touch and taste are all involved in sexual arousal. In addition imagination is as effective a stimulus as reality and on occasion suggestiveness is a more erotic stimulus than naked presence.

There is a pattern of sexual arousal in any given individual which is personal to him or her and which is dependent on a complex interaction of biological, sociological and psychological factors. It cannot be denied for instance, that some 'gentlemen prefer blondes', nor that some women are bowled over by men who 'walk tall' while others are repelled by the smell of 'strong, husky men'. There is, however, in addition to purely personal preferences and repulsions, an observable general difference between the ways in which people of different sex respond to erotic stimuli. It is known that in general men respond

27

to erotic visual stimuli more readily than women. It is also known that women are more able to detect musk smells than are men, and, that women are erotically aroused more easily by taste, hearing and touch stimuli than by visual material. These facts would probably not surprise anyone who sells 'girlie' magazines, or who courts a woman, but pioneering work by Le Magnan in 1950, and later by Garai and Scheinfeld among others, have confirmed these observations through controlled experiments. Their work has shown that these different responses of men and women are hormonally based and in women subject to fluctuations at different times in the menstrual cycle.[11]

The important role of the hormones in sexual arousal is reinforced by socio-psychological factors such as memorable events in early childhood experience. Children often discover the pleasure of self-stimulation during their play. Their natural curiosity about one another's bodies helps them to find out what kinds of play give themselves and other children intense pleasure and satisfaction. As they grow up many of them make an important link between their sexual feelings and romantic love through the passionate experience of hero worship for historical figures, story-book characters or living people whom they either know or come into contact with through the media. Nor is it only young people who live vicariously through the achievements of personal heroes and heroines. Many adults study the fortunes of particular individuals and imagine themselves living like the people whom they so much admire. Their attachment to their hero or heroine is romantic although some of them are unaware of any physical sexual involvement because they have repressed or sublimated their sexual feelings. They transfer these feelings to ordinary mortals who cross their paths: initially, at least, they may be able to form very satisfactory relationships with quite ordinary people on this romantic basis. Previous sexual arousals form patterns in people's memories which form the basis for future relationships; so old

28

experiences can enhance or hinder the development of new sexual friendships.

Apart from biological factors and socio-psychological 'imprinting' or 'patterning', which affect people's ability to respond to sexual stimuli, there are some important moral factors which influence people's behaviour. Human beings derive much of their moral code from their parents, immediate peers and the general moral climate of the society in which they live, so that to some extent their moral-value systems are based on socio-psychological foundations. But morality depends not only upon a community's code of practice but also upon its members' ability to evaluate and choose a way of life which is consistent with their own religious beliefs, some of which may be held in direct opposition to established social conventions. During their early years, the Mormons, for instance, embraced polygamy and so they came into open conflict with the established Christian tradition of monogamy. Mormon moral codes operated within their own society even though their community was surrounded by people who had a different way of looking at sex, sexual arousal and sexual behaviour, and whose sanctions and rewards for good and bad moral behaviour differed from those of the Mormons. Pioneer Mormons were guided primarily by their religious beliefs which may have operated in harmony with their hormones but which certainly did not accord with the expectations of the culture in which they lived. Consequently, Mormons became a tight-knit community with distinctive customs and laws which fostered a particular attitude towards sexuality, until the weakening of religious fervour, together with cultural intermingling, led to an erosion of their numerical strength and a subsequent change in their attitude towards polygamy. In a different context, the same kind of religious dilemma confronts minority Christian communities who develop among polygamous societies. Christian leaders have succeeded in getting their early converts to adhere to monogamy for the sake of their religion for a time, but they have found it well-nigh impossible to impose a continuing monogamous tradition in an environment where the prevailing religious beliefs, moral codes and patterns of sexual behaviour continue to be designed for an established polygamous society.

People's religious and moral attitudes sometimes inhibit inappropriate sexual responses because certain otherwise desirable objects of affection are seen to be forbidden for good reasons. The objects become taboo. Hence the incest taboo prevents most parents and children from experiencing overt sexual desire for each other. The taboo enables them to live together with a minimum of difficulty. It also operates strongly between siblings so that although brothers and sisters may feel sexually aroused by each other they automatically look outside their immediate family for their sexual partners.

Taboos are usually effective but they can break down whenever a forbidden stimulus evokes an inappropriate response. The failure of sexual taboos to operate properly may result in incest, pederasty and some types of fetishism, and these conditions may bring people to counsellors for help.

Although much is now known about the many different factors involved in sexual arousal it is still a matter of controversy as to whether or not the sexual arousal systems of the human body operate in the same way for homosexuals as for heterosexuals. There is also much argument about the differences between men's and women's sexual responses during sexual intercourse. Seeing that there is so much uncertainty and controversy about the many ways in which people are roused by and respond to sexual stimuli, it is quite a relief to realize that the urge to find sexual satisfaction is common to all human beings whatever their sexual orientation, although again there can be no doubt but that there are wide variations in people's sexual drive, potency and ability to achieve sexual satisfaction, especially if those who are engaged in sexual intercourse are also seeking spiritual and psychological fulfilment as well as bodily pleasure.

Sex, self and fulfilment

Some people appear to think of their sexuality in rather negative terms. They seem to be content to achieve relief from sexual tension through sexual activity of various kinds. They deny that sexual behaviour should be related to romantic love. It is easy to be cynical about sex, especially in western society where so much emphasis is placed upon sexual conquest, prowess and physical organs and so little on the importance of love in relationships, whether or not they are sexual. However, whenever individuals are asked about their deepest desires for themselves, most of them will still say that they want to use the gift of sexuality in ways which will bring them happiness and fulfilment, either by living alone or in close partnership with another person or several people. Some men and women live contentedly without engaging in any obvious outward sexual activity, but the majority form sexual partnerships with other people with varying degrees of success.

An individual's chance of finding personal happiness and fulfilment is enhanced if she or he can enjoy being sexually aroused and achieving orgasm without guilt. This delight in sexual pleasure is intimately bound up with people's understanding of their own identity, sexuality and personal destiny. Anyone who works as a counsellor quickly learns how much individual suffering is caused by ignorance about sex in all its aspects, by judgements about sexual behaviour which are based upon an inadequate understanding of the relationship between sex and 'self', and by self-denigration and guilt at having sexual desires and needs at all. Some of this suffering is the direct result of past erroneous religious thinking.

Religion is a sensitive subject because it touches people's

deepest and most private feelings about themselves. This is why many counsellors feel it right to refrain from talking about a client's religious attitudes until a good rapport has been established between them. Nevertheless, counsellors who are aware of their own religious attitudes towards sex can often perceive similar unspoken attitudes at work in their clients. A sensitive approach towards one's own and other people's religious beliefs can be very helpful as it often enables a counsellor to discuss previously acquired negative or positive attitudes which may be operating destructively or constructively within a person. Sometimes a therapeutic relationship can result in a real change of the balance between negative and positive religious attitudes in both counsellor and client so that one or both of them become able to develop a more creative approach towards the particular problem under consideration.

This sensitivity towards religious belief is especially important in regard to western-Christian attitudes towards sex and sexual relationships. The Christian Church has to accept considerable responsibility for people's misconceptions and prejudices about sex, sexuality and sexual activity since in the past much of its teaching has been based upon an ignorance of biological facts and an inadequate understanding of psychology, anthropology and the social sciences. Christian theologians have been slow to modify their theories about sex and sexuality in the light of scientific discovery, and too many of them appear to have been unconsciously influenced by dualism so that they have tended to think of sexual intercourse as an earthy and potentially sinful activity and of sexual abstinence as a godly and spiritual exercise. It is possible, of course, to find thousands of examples to prove that many Christian attitudes towards human sexuality have been more positive than that, but, again, they have tended to be positive only within the strictly defined limits of heterosexual 'normality', marriage or total chastity. They have remained negative towards all other expressions of sexuality such as homosexual activity and all extra-marital sexual behaviour.

These negative or partially negative religious attitudes are still at work today and they can have an adverse effect on people's lives, but happily there are signs that more positive attitudes are developing. Many Christians do now see sex as a God-given gift to all human beings irrespective of their constitution, identity, aptitudes and appetites. They believe that sex is good and that sexuality should contribute to personal growth. They also think that the way in which human beings use their God-given sexuality determines whether their actions are constructive or destructive, good or evil, godly or ungodly, but they do not necessarily judge behaviour by previously accepted criteria. Instead they look for new ways of looking at sexual relationships and new approaches towards dealing with people's sexual problems, and some of these new approaches will be considered in later chapters of this book.

TWO
Sexual Relationships

People who are used to thinking of the family as a stabilizing force in society and of marriage as a passport to individual happiness are sometimes tempted to think that most people could be 'normal' heterosexuals, capable of living with one marriage partner and of rearing happy healthy children if only they were committed to the old ideal of lifelong marriage. Those who look at the family in this way tend to be nostalgic about the past, when dedicated celibacy was considered to be the only possible alternative to marriage, and they look hopefully to countries like Spain or Ireland where Church and State still uphold marriage and celibacy by forbidding legal divorce. It is, in fact, doubtful that life was, or is, any happier for the men and women who had, or still have, to grow up and live in those kinds of restrictive society than it is for those who are growing to maturity in a modern post-Christian society in the western world, and this kind of nostalgic thinking may simply reflect the way in which people's emotions can become overburdened as they hear about the problems of others and struggle to cope with their own.

Counsellors run a special risk of developing a rather jaundiced view of sex because so many of their clients seem to have difficulties with tangled sexual relationships. They may need to remind themselves from time to time that the great majority of people never come to seek their help because they do not experience any major problems in their personal relationships. Just as most people learn to eat and drink according to their bodily needs, so most men and women learn to strike a reasonably happy balance between sexual appetite and sexual satisfaction.

Sexual starvation and sexual gluttony certainly affect most people's lives on occasion, but they do not become a major problem unless under- or over-indulgence in sexual activity is symptomatic of disordered intra-psychic or inter-personal relationships. This means that disturbances of sexual appetite or function do not necessarily cause sufficient distress to merit correction. Every counsellor, for instance, will come across partnerships between men and women where sexual intercourse either never takes place or is very infrequent, and yet the couple are genuinely happy to be married to each other because they are great friends. Similarly, but at the other end of the scale, there are a number of marriage partners who consider themselves to be happily married although they know that their spouses have 'affairs' outside the marriage. They positively welcome the relief of not having to keep up with their partner's pace. There are also some people of average sexual appetite and potency who make a deliberate choice to remain celibate. Although these people may feel sexually frustrated at times they do not regard such frustration as unhealthy—and they are right, for the frequency of sexual activity or degree of inactivity should never be used as the only way of measuring normality or health. Wholeness is a concept that cannot be defined by such narrow criteria.

On the other hand, quite minor symptoms of sexual frustration, over-indulgence or other disorder may point to gravely disturbed relationships. This is a well-known fact, but it is all too easy for clients and counsellors alike to allow minor presenting problems to occupy their attention so that they may overlook more serious trouble behind the obvious symptoms.

People bring all kinds of sexual problem to counsellors. The art of counselling depends on a counsellor's ability to recognize the reality of these problems and to know their significance in the lives of those who confide in him or her in the hope that their problems can be solved and their disturbed relationships sorted out.

It is sometimes difficult to write about problems of sexual relationship because it is tempting either to treat a problem as if it were too rare to be shared by anyone else, or to deal with it as if it were a commonplace difficulty to which a universal solution could be applied. People do not manufacture their problems on a mass-production line, nor do counsellors deal with problems in a generalized way, for they know that each client is an individual with a unique problem which calls for a particular solution within a specific context. Nevertheless, case histories can sometimes usefully illustrate the kinds of difficulty which occur in real life because many people do share the same kinds of problem, and it is possible to discern in their stories some of the underlying principles of their treatment which might help counsellors and clients to find solutions in other similar but not identical problems.

Sexual isolates

The first group of people who come to mind as having difficulties in establishing good sexual relationships are the sexual isolates. They are well represented by Alice, a middle-aged lady who had never been asked to be anyone's sexual partner.

Alice's parents had lived in a small village on the sea coast where they kept a general store which doubled as the local post office. Alice was their only child and she was greatly loved. It seemed quite natural to everyone in the village that she should take over the shop as her parents grew older. She looked after them devotedly. Alice was forty-five years old before she found herself living quite alone.

When her parents had been alive Alice had never minded being a spinster. She had been too busy to pay much attention to her sexual needs, but now she had less to do she began to notice men's bodies. She watched television avidly and to her horror noticed her own interest in the bulging jeans worn by some actors. She felt the physical discomfort of an engorged clitoris. She knew little about the physical changes in her body and even less about their meaning so her efforts to describe them to her doctor only resulted in a prescription for tranquillizers which did not help her at all. In desperation she confided her problem to a friend who told her how to release the tension in her body through self-stimulation, but Alice felt too guilty about masturbation to indulge in it very often. Then she took her problem to her vicar but she was too shy to explain herself properly.

The vicar did his best although he did not quite understand Alice's oblique references to her sexual problem. He realized how lonely she must be so he suggested that she might like to come to the Wednesday afternoon women's fellowship. In the hope of making her feel useful he asked her to look after their monthly raffle. After all, he said, it would be very easy for someone who ran a shop as efficiently as she did, to run a monthly raffle for a ladies' meeting. Alice agreed to his request. She felt it would be ungrateful for her to refuse. But she felt imprisoned by her body and trapped by her inability to speak about her problem openly or to solve it by herself.

Alice knew that she ought to try to find men friends of her own age but she could not bring herself to do that, nor did she go to the Wednesday afternoon meetings as she had promised to do. Her sense of isolation increased. Her guilty secret haunted her. She became depressed and, when that feeling became the dominant feature of her life, she noticed with relief that her sexual problem had disappeared.

Alice had temporarily solved her problem through becoming ill, but obviously it was not the best way of dealing with her difficulties. It is easy to see how she could have been helped if only she had been able to bring her anxieties out into the open, but the relief of confiding in another person would not have helped her to find a marriage partner unless she had also been very fortunate in her encounters with eligible men.

Alice's problem is not uncommon, nor is it confined to middle-aged women. Men who find it difficult to take the initiative in making sexual contacts may also become isolated. People who find themselves sexually impotent on one occasion may prefer to remain alone rather than attempt intercourse again and risk failure. Some of the women and men who become sexual isolates appear to be happily married or well matched with their sexual partner, but they do not enjoy sexual intercourse nor do they find it easy to discuss their difficulties with their current partners. People may love each other deeply and yet be unable to be open with each other for fear of causing mutual pain, so they accept isolation rather than attempt dialogue. People who become isolated in this way can become very lonely, and the loneliness may drive them to seek happiness outside their stable relationships, as the story of Eric and Julie's marriage shows.

Eric and Julie were a happily married couple with three children, all of whom were at school. Eric was an office worker, and at the time their trouble began, Julie had recently found part-time work in a local factory near their home.

Their sexual relationship had never been ecstatic but it was quite adequate until after the birth of their third child, when Julie began to find herself reluctant to have sexual intercourse. At first, she found a good reason for her indifference, for their new baby needed a lot of attention and Julie felt tired most of the time. Later, when she could no longer justify her reluctance in this way, she began to pretend that she enjoyed Eric's amorous advances rather than disappoint him. Initially she was thankful that Eric did not appear to notice the difference between her simulated pleasure and real orgasm, but quite soon she began to resent his insensitivity. She became tense and irritable with her husband and children. Eric blamed her unpleasant temper on her factory work and urged her to give it up. Julie resisted this idea fiercely since she liked her job, needed the money and enjoyed the freedom it gave her.

Once or twice she tried to talk to Eric about her problem. Unfortunately, on the one occasion when they managed to have a real discussion about sexual intercourse she fastened on their relative inability to reach their sexual climax at the same time and Eric felt that she was blaming him for her fault. His self-esteem was damaged and he snapped back at her with a totally unjustifiable criticism. It took them both a long time to get over their hurt feelings, and neither of them wanted to risk another argument on those lines.

After that incident Julie felt more lonely than ever. She began to think that she no longer loved her husband and family and

38

she started to look to other relationships for sexual adventure. She was an attractive woman, so it was not long before she found herself a man whose sexual approach was novel enough to excite her interest. Shortly afterwards she walked out of her home.

Eric was devastated. He could not understand what had happened. Julie's inability to share her feelings with him had given him no real chance of breaking through her loneliness so that he could have tried to put things right between them. His own failure to accept painful criticism had given his wife no chance of telling him how guilty she felt about her frigidity. Neither of them had found a way to tell the other how much they had really loved each other. Their marriage breakdown was tragic, not only for themselves, but for their children and for society as a whole.

Eric and Julie's story, as well as Alice's, shows that people who are sexually isolated and lonely often share an inability to recognize the depth of their own frustration, or to talk about it, even to those who love them and whom they love and trust. They often seem to be ashamed of admitting their need for sexual satisfaction. This means that counsellors who are consulted by sexual isolates will need to be specially patient and sensitive if they are to help some of their clients to reveal their feelings. Confession nearly always reduces the clients' sense of loneliness. Sometimes it enables them to break through the psychological barriers which prevent them from forming satisfying personal relationships. Some people who have good insight into their own problems, however, must remain unhealed because their condition is permanent, usually because of physical illness. In a moving passage in a book called *Free Fall* a dying woman, JoAnn Kelley Smith, refers to her feelings about her relationship with her husband which is dying as she herself nears death. She says:

At the age of forty-seven his sex drives continue to be normal. Mine are gone. Gail and Paula sense his vulnerability and become over-protective of any kind of contact he has with women, often our mutual friends. He assures me even though that part of our relationship is over, the depth of love he has for me has not diminished. But our sexual relationship has always been an important part of our marriage, and because its mutual enjoyment is gone, I now realize death has come to another area of human existence that made life so good for me. It is lost in my free fall. This has become another source of my deep depression.[1]

It is quite possible to be loved as JoAnn was and yet feel sexually isolated. It is equally possible to live alone and yet escape any sense of being walled off from other people. Indeed, some people choose to live alone as a way of expressing their love for others. The creative potential of the solitary life will be discussed in a later chapter. It is mentioned here only because it is important to be able to recognize which clients need help and which simply need to be reassured that they are living their lives in ways that are right for them. The creative solitary life is marked by a deep sense of joy which is a source of inspiration to others, whereas sexual isolation is a condition bringing misery to many people besides the person immediately involved.

A number of people who become sexually isolated, for whatever reason, will decide to accept their suffering rather than face what they feel to be the even greater suffering which might come to them through overt sexual behaviour and involvement with other people.

Sexual Involvement

Since human beings are sexual beings their sexuality is involved in all their activity, whether it be withdrawal from emotional relationships or engagement in overt sexual behaviour. Within the context of this chapter about people's sexual relationships and some of the problems which arise because of them, sexual involvement is taken to mean genital sexual involvement with oneself or another person.

Men and women become aware of sexual feelings in their

bodily organs whenever they respond to sexual stimuli which may come from within their own imaginations or from outside themselves. These feelings are intensely pleasurable unless the object of desire is a forbidden one, when a psychological mechanism will veto the feelings before they have expressed themselves openly. The mechanism which prevents sexual desire from being translated into sexual behaviour may come into play because of a self-imposed ban, a rejection from the desirable object or because of strong communal disapproval. When all these factors coexist relatively few people will have any difficulty in controlling their feelings towards the forbidden objects of desire. Many people, for instance, may admire the beauty of young children's bodies, but they train themselves not to respond sexually to the sight of naked or half-clothed children because they do not want to be sexually aroused in this way. They respect the innocence of children and their feelings are inhibited by the general revulsion in society against any active sexual behaviour which involves children. Similar inhibitory mechanisms prevent most people from sexual involvement with animals, members of their own family and, to a lesser extent, with close friends who are already sexually committed to other people.

In all these instances sexual desire is usually nipped in the bud before it can be translated into overt sexual behaviour, but sometimes the intra-psychic veto mechanism fails. When that happens a few people simply respond to their sexual urges and seem to be able to enjoy themselves without guilt. In many people, however, a tug of war develops between their desire for sexual gratification and their consciences.

Guilt feelings vary in intensity according to circumstances and individual temperament. They are heavily influenced by people's moral upbringing and by the currently accepted moral standards of society. Guilt is a very unpleasant sensation so it is not surprising that many people try to escape it by avoiding any sexual behaviour which steps outside the boundaries which they consider to be legitimate.

Guilt may initially be a relatively efficient emotion in securing a person's good behaviour, but it has less restraining power in the presence of strong sexual desire which is persistent, especially when the sexually roused person is presented with a good opportunity of obtaining the desired relief from sexual tension. Since sexual desire is a very powerful driving force quite capable of overriding rational thought, many women and men find themselves involved in a variety of sexual contacts and behaviour which go against the dictates of their consciences to a greater or lesser extent. Anyone who has struggled with strong sexual desire and given in to it will know that persistent failure to control sexual feelings can become a problem, and it is this kind of situation which often brings people to counsellors for help.

Sexual self-stimulation

Most young people know what it is like to feel sexually roused. In modern western society adolescent sexual fantasy and self-stimulation to the point of orgasm are widely accepted as a normal feature of human development, although the Roman Catholic Church still regards such behaviour as sinful, at any rate in its official teaching. The changed social attitudes of the majority of people towards sexual self-stimulation or masturbation, has brought peace of mind to many people who now feel that their sexual appetites can be treated like any other appetite. Just as they recognize their human need to eat and drink, but do not wish to starve themselves nor to gorge themselves, so they can admit to their need for sexual pleasure without wishing to suppress it completely or to enslave themselves to its delights.

Most young people learn about sexual self-stimulation

through handling their own bodies, or from other boys and girls.

Many young people deepen their understanding of their sexuality and themselves through learning to explore their own bodies and being able to enjoy orgasm. Such sexual activity need not be tainted by guilt and self-disgust. It is a great deal safer and less traumatic than premature or casual sexual intercourse. People can learn to treat their own bodies and needs with the tenderness and reverence they deserve. Masturbation is not a necessary activity for everyone but it can and often does lead to healthy attitudes towards natural bodily functions. As they grow older most young people pass quite easily from masturbation into the greater pleasure of sexual partnership. They will generally only return to self-stimulation for relief of sexual tension when they are deprived of their usual partners for some time.

Masturbation, however, does have its negative aspects. Some people find that self-stimulation produces orgasm more quickly and easily than does sexual intercourse and they may find themselves in considerable difficulty because of this discovery. Lionel's case history illustrates this very real problem.

Lionel had always enjoyed sex. During adolescence he had experimented with himself and other boys. Later on, he had two or three lighthearted affairs with girl friends until he married Mary and 'settled down'.

Lionel enjoyed his life with Mary and they had three children before she developed multiple sclerosis. Despite good medical care the disease progressed rapidly. Mary soon lost the ability to control her arms and legs, and her paralysis made it impossible for her to enjoy sexual intimacy with Lionel in the same way as before. She was always comforted when he told her that he loved her and was still sexually roused by her. He would curl up beside her and fondle her body and his own until he had an orgasm. Although Mary rarely shared the same pleasure, she was always happy for him, so they continued to make love to each other in this way until her death some fifteen years after the onset of her illness.

43

Lionel mourned his wife for two years. He went on obtaining relief from sexual tension by manual self-stimulation, as he found this a simple and acceptable way of dealing with his sexual needs. By now he was fifty-five years old, and he did not expect to remarry. So he was quite surprised when he fell in love with a widow who was five years younger than himself.

Their relationship flourished, and they were married within six months.

It was then that Lionel discovered that he was impotent when it came to sexual intercourse. He was stimulated by Marianne and he could help her to have orgasm but he was quite unable to maintain an erection or achieve penetration. On the other hand he was able to reach orgasm if he fondled himself when he was alone. He and Marianne were distressed enough to seek medical help.

The doctor to whom they went could find no physical cause for Lionel's symptoms. He decided that Lionel had grown so used to masturbation as a way of reaching orgasm that he had lost the knack of sexual intercourse. So he sent Lionel to a behavioural psychologist who helped Lionel to retrain his body's response to sexual stimuli so that he could enjoy being touched and pleasured by his new wife. Lionel and Marianne enjoyed their sensate focus training and eventually learnt how to obtain mutual satisfaction through varied ways of making love to each other.

Lionel's case study illustrates one way in which self-stimulation can cause real problems for men and women when it interferes with their ability to engage in and enjoy sexual intercourse with a partner of their choice.

Masturbation can also be a problem to people who feel morally guilty about their use of it to secure relief from sexual tension. People acquire many of their attitudes towards masturbation from their parents and older people in society. Until quite recently most people thought that masturbation could be harmful to physical and psychological health. Nowadays most scientists reject the idea that masturbation is harmful, but old fears and superstitions die hard. Many parents still discourage their

44

children from touching intimate parts of their bodies by making them feel guilty whenever they show any open interest in their genital organs. Children who have been exposed to this kind of parental disapproval will commonly associate masturbation with guilty feelings.

Some people disapprove of any form of sexual self-stimulation on religious grounds. Such sincere beliefs must be treated seriously whenever anyone feels guilty about masturbation. Guilt torments people and they may seek help from counsellors who do not share their religious or moral beliefs. Counsellors must respect their clients' beliefs even if they do not share them.

Clients and counsellors have to decide for themselves which attitudes to adopt to the problem of guilt over self-stimulation. Counsellors can give emotional support to their clients who are learning to stop masturbation in order to be able to live with a quiet conscience. Alternatively, clients can be encouraged to accept the relief of masturbation either by learning to tolerate their guilt, or by rejecting the official teaching of their religious organizations, so freeing themselves from guilt. Both these approaches are valid ones, and the choice of which one to use in a particular case must depend upon the moral beliefs held by the clients and counsellors as well as the circumstances which bring them together.

Self-stimulation does not cause people so much un-happiness as it did a generation or two ago, so fewer people seek help from a counsellor for this reason. Instead, problems which arise in connection with sexual fantasies are more frequently discussed openly as they cause many people a good deal of distress.

Sexual fantasies

Sexual self-stimulation may be a self-absorbing physical activity. More commonly it is a solitary activity in response to an imagined sexual object such as another person, a fetish or an animal. The sexual appetite can be stimulated through any or all of the senses, or through the power of the brain to create its own mental images. Suggestive advertisements, half-clothed people, a sensual voice, or a song which evokes memories, are all typical stimuli which can precipitate strong sexual urges in human beings, especially in those who are hungry for sexual contact or whose sexual needs are above average. The imagination, with its capacity to convey idealized pictures of the beloved person, idol or desired object, is often a more powerful sexual stimulus than reality and this seems particularly true for those who are too shy to make personal contact with other people.

Sexual fantasies are part of human experience. They occur in women and men alike. Although it used to be thought that women fantasized less than men it is now known that this is true only with regard to visual fantasies, and recent accounts of women's sexual fantasies have revealed the extent to which fantasy is important in the sexual experiences of women.[2]

Fantasies are indeed so universal that many people are unaware of their strength and importance in western commercial life. Manufacturers, for instance, often design their advertisements to appeal to men's and women's fantasies about themselves. Potential purchasers are bombarded with an astonishing array of sensual stimuli in an attempt to persuade them to buy the various goods on offer. Many of these advertisements imply that the customer will become more sexually attractive or potent if she or he buys the goods which the advertisers want to sell. Unfortunately for western society, the manufacturers have overloaded the public imagination, and appetites have become jaded. People lose their ability to respond to sexual stimuli which are too obvious or too familiar. This fact may be one of the most important reasons for the proliferation of sado-masochistic and pornographic images in advertising. The use of stronger images may titillate the imaginations of some people, but it revolts others and probably debases all human beings along the way.

Although many people may not be aware of the extent to which they are involved in the communal fantasy life of their own community through advertisements and strongly portrayed media images of 'pin-up' idols, most people are familiar with their own private fantasies. They are quite happy to indulge in harmless day-dreams from time to time. They enjoy identifying themselves with some of the larger-than-life characters whom they meet in novels, plays, films and television shows. It is only when sexual images preoccupy their attention to the exclusion of almost everything else that they begin to worry about their fantasies.

People respond in a variety of different ways to their obsessive sexual ruminations. Some pursue their dream objects indefatigably. They seldom find a satisfactory sexual partner because no real person can match up to their idol. Some people devote an excessive amount of time exposing themselves to sensual stimuli. They may become balletomaines, constant theatre and cinema goers, compulsive gamblers, fanatic pet lovers, ardent religious devotees.

Other men and women become more openly and obviously involved in their sexual fantasies. They may become consumers of sexual novels, films and plays by the dozen. They may haunt sex shops, strip shows and brothels. They may buy pornographic material. Some people even use their creative talents in the service of pornographic art and literature. There are also a number of people who try to expunge their own obsessive fantasies by zealously attacking them within their own minds and in society as a whole.

Many of these ways of dealing with the fantasy world are adequate for their purpose, but a number of people become disturbed by their fantasies and it is these people who are likely to ask for help from relatives, friends or professional counsellors.

People who are worried by their obsessive sexual thoughts are often very shy about them, so they tend to approach their problem in an indirect way by asking for advice about an associated symptom instead of mentioning their real worry. This means that counsellors may have to do some detective work before they can find the real cause of their client's malaise. As with most sexual problems, difficulties over sexual fantasies can be confided to another person only if there is a good rapport between counsellor and client, and this may take some time to establish. When, however, the self-revelation does take place it is often catharic, and the emotional relief can be lasting. The fantasies may disappear altogether. They may lessen their stranglehold, or they may become part of a reality-based relationship. If the obsessive thoughts become more compelling, counsellors and clients should look for more serious underlying causes.

Sexual fantasies can occur in some forms of organic brain disease like tumours and epilepsy. They can also disturb people who suffer from some kinds of obsessional neurosis, manic-depressive psychosis and schizophrenia. These fantasies are often more vivid and bizarre than those which are due to repressed sexual energy. They may be so fixed in the imagination that they can be said to be delusions or hallucinations which blot out reality.

These kinds of sexual fantasies do not respond to the kind of healing situation which results from their open confession to an accepting and understanding confidant. Sexual fantasies which come from an organic brain disease or psychotic illness respond only when the underlying disease is actively treated with surgery, drugs or electro-convulsive therapy. Counsellors who meet clients with fixed fantasies need to be aware of their possible origin and to refrain from determined and repeated attempts to banish them by discussion, confession or exorcism. If they

48

make a mistake and treat them as sinful or demonic in origin they may add to their client's burden and contribute to a situation which may end in disaster for all concerned.

Experienced priests, counsellors and psychiatrists know the dangers of being caught in their clients' fantasies. They are aware of the possibility of slipping into a *folie-à-deux* situation so that they come to share and believe in their clients' fantasies. These dangers can be avoided if counsellors are willing to seek outside help when they run into resistent fantasies and bizarre ruminations. It is true that very ill patients are seldom treated as if they were sinners or demon possessed, but mistakes do happen, largely because of counsellors' misguided attempts to deal with problems without expert medical help. Counsellors may not wish to betray the confidence of their clients, but it is, after all, quite possible for them to discuss their clients' problems with outsiders if they first obtain permission to do so, or to talk about them theoretically if they cannot secure consent. Such discussions will almost invariably reveal the dangers of a situation in which the counsellors may be unwittingly trapped.

Sexual relationships with oneself and sexual relationships with one's fantasies are important areas of human experience and cannot be neglected by counsellors who are interested in sexual relationships, but, on the whole, they will meet these problems less often than those which arise through unsatisfactory sexual intercourse.

Sexual intercourse

Most Christians agree that commercial western attitudes towards sexual intercourse are unhealthy. Men and women are constantly urged by the media to seek perfection in their sexual relationships with their sexual partners. Perfection seems to be equated with simultaneous mutual arousal, strong erection, complete receptivity, reciprocal and equal pleasure and pulsating orgasm achieved by both partners at the same time. Such perfection could be achieved by machines programmed to operate efficiently in a repetitive fashion, but human beings are not machines and they do not function in this way unless they lose some of their humanity.

When unrealistic goals are abandoned sexual intercourse between two people becomes an intimate exploration on which they embark without knowing precisely where they are going but knowing that they want to share their journey. When the adventure is mutually satisfying all is well, but unfortunately sexual difficulties and malfunctions do occur, and they can cause much misery if they remain undiagnosed or untreated.

Sexual intercourse can go wrong because of mechanical failures. The sexual organs may be faulty. Alternatively, the controlling central nervous and autonomic nervous systems which control the functioning of people's bodies during sexual intercourse may not be functioning properly. It is usually relatively easy to discover whether or not the cause of sexual dysfunction lies in the organs themselves, in the hormonal endocrine system or the nervous system which controls the endocrines and genital organs.

The counsellor's first task is to establish where the trouble is coming from and then to refer clients to the appropriate specialists where necessary. Counsellors will always find a sizeable residuum of clients in whom no obvious mechanical failure can be found and in whom the psychosexual nervous pathways are intact, but who continue to experience difficulties in sexual intercourse.

When counsellors have excluded diseased organs or malfunctions in the endocrine and nervous systems as possible causes of their clients' malaise they have to decide whether or not the difficulties of which their clients complain are serious psychosocial problems or variations of the normal.

Many people, including the author, now believe that no one sexual orientation can be thought to be any more 'normal' than another, so in this context heterosexual, homosexual and bisexual practices are considered together rather than separately.

Sexual intercourse is such a personal and intimate human experience that it is impossible to assert that people can be considered to be normal only if they have sexual relations with their partners in particular ways. Nevertheless, during the course of their work counsellors will meet hundreds of people who will ask them for reassurance about the normality of their sexual behaviour.

The story of Mary Jane illustrates the kind of problems which clients bring to counsellors when they are worried about their normality.

Mary Jane was a forty-year-old married woman with three children. She had completed her family when she was thirty-five years old and had used oral contraceptives ever since. During one of her routine family-planning examinations she suddenly told the doctor of her anxieties about her sexual relationship with her husband.

It seemed that ever since their marriage twenty years before there had been times when her husband had insisted on going though a complicated preamble to sexual intercourse during which he liked to bind her arms to her body before forcing her legs apart in order to have sexual intercourse. She had accepted his need for this ritual and had found that some resistence on her part had in fact heightened his pleasure. Mary Jane and her husband were regular church attenders and she had felt guilty about these episodes, but she had never dared to talk about them before.

She asked the doctor whether her husband was normal, and whether she was conniving at sin by consenting to his desire in this way? She also wondered whether they could be helped to stop this kind of sexual intercourse?

A detailed history established the fact that Mary Jane quite enjoyed bondage and that her main concern was to see whether or not she and her husband had substituted orgiastic games for real love. She was worried in case they should come to despise each other and discover that they no longer loved each other. Her real need was to be reassured by her husband that she was loved by him as much as ever, but since she did not dare to ask that question of someone for whom she cared very deeply, she had come to the doctor as a second-best alternative.

The doctor's reactions to Mary Jane's questions helped her to turn away from comparing herself and her husband with other people. She was set free from her anxieties about 'normality' and encouraged to look for signs of love in her marital relationship. She was able to find these quite easily, and she was then able to ask her husband for the reassurance which she longed for, and which he readily gave her once he realized what she needed.

Mary Jane's story is fairly typical of many consultations about sexual problems. Clients like her often ask questions about their intimate problems during a conversation about some other matter. They can talk about their anxieties only at times which are right for them, even though such moments may be very inconvenient for the counsellors. Many people ask for reassurance at a superficial level when they really need help with a deeper unspoken anxiety which they cannot easily bring out into the open. Clients like Mary Jane often ask counsellors questions which they dare not ask of close relatives. So counsellors need to listen to their clients with ears which can tune in to what is not said as well as to what they are told. They must be ready to help their clients at a deep level. At the same time they should remember that many clients can be helped by straightforward answers to direct questions. A lot of these direct questions are asked by people who want to know if they are normal or abnormal human beings.

Many people are still very ignorant about sexual behaviour. A lot of fears about themselves can disappear once they can accept the idea that many different kinds of sexual behaviour can be 'normal'. They then realize that it is useless for them to compare themselves with other people. They can then measure their behaviour against the yardstick of their own moral conscience which can be influenced, but not dominated, by other people's standards of behaviour.

It is encouraging to know that many people can be reassured about their sexual normality simply by talking about themselves to somebody else who helps them to accept themselves as they are. Many people, for instance, stop being anxious about the size of their external organs when they can be reassured that function and pleasure are more important than size and appearance. Many men with small genitals come to realize that they are as virile as men with large organs. Small-breasted women can learn that they may be very attractive despite their self-consciousness about physical appearance which makes them feel estranged from the majority of their sex. These and similar anxieties about physical sexual characteristics are, however, less important than anxieties about sexual performance.

People worry a great deal about their sexual performance during intercourse, and so long as they continue to compare themselves with other men and women they will continue to feel anxious. When they adopt a different standard of 'normality' their fears disappear. Many clients find that they are relieved of their anxiety if they are told that their behaviour is normal when it is mutually acceptable to the people involved, leads to sexual fulfilment and encourages the growth of love between the partners. This standard of normality does not seek to compare the couple with other people in similar circumstances. Instead, the point of reference is the relationship between the two people who are relating sexually to each other. This internal reference point helps each partner to take the needs of the other into consideration. It encourages them to look at themselves as a pair, both of whom have sexual needs and rights over the other, both of whom seek mutual happiness and fulfilment. It also takes into account the concept that sexual intercourse is part of a loving relationship but is not the essence of it.

This last point about sexual intercourse is an important one which is often lost sight of because it is quite possible to separate sexual intercourse from loving intercourse, to view sexual intercourse as a physiological response to a mechanical stimulus which exists on its own and which has no necessary relationship to affection or love. In *Proposals for a New Sexual Ethic* Dr J. Dominian explains how this kind of mental separation takes place. He says:

The experience of touching, watching, talking and listening are the foundations of physical intimacy, the infrastructure of human attachment and therefore of affection. Later on after puberty the very same experiences will be capable of arousing not only affection but also sexual desire. Furthermore sexual arousal can now occur in the absence of any personal attachment, friendship or love. It can be simply a sexual drive or in other terms a lustful longing without any bonds of affection towards the person with whom the sexual arousal is experienced.

There is little doubt in my mind that here is the key to the fear attached to human sexuality, namely the severance at puberty between genital sex and any necessary attachment to the object of the sexual arousal, the essence of prostitution and one of the symbols in the Old Testament of Israel's unfaithfulness to Yahweh. No one denies this crucial human predicament but because it exists there is no reason to devalue either human affection or sexuality in the presence of a loving relationship.[3]

Many people have some experience of the way in which genital sex can get separated from love. Young women and men often 'sow their wild oats'. Many people are promiscuous on occasion. Most know what it is to feel 'randy'. Yet, whenever people are asked what they hope for from sexual intercourse, they nearly always imply that they value it as a way of establishing and maintaining a relationship of love. That is why the ability to make love and to respond to another person's sexual interest is so important to so many people. Their self-esteem is closely bound up with their sexual performance. Any real or imagined failure in sexual performance can lead to a sense of sexual inadequacy which can be quite devastating.

Sexual inadequacy

Sexual inadequacy of one kind or another brings many people to counsellors. Indeed, this kind of problem is often precipitated by fear alone. Many people who are afraid of becoming inadequate do become inadequate. This kind of sexual malfunctioning is so common among those who consult professional counsellors that Masters and Johnson used italics to emphasize their point when they wrote about it in their classic book on sexual inadequacy:

It should be restated that fear of inadequacy is the greatest known deterrent to effective sexual functioning simply because it so completely distracts the fearful individual from his or her natural responsivity by blocking reception of sexual stimuli either created by or reflected from the sexual partner.[4]

Fear is one important cause of sexual inadequacy. Self-rejection is another cause of inadequacy. Some people do not feel worthy to enjoy sensual pleasure or ecstasy. They may feel guilty at having sexual feelings at all. They may hate themselves because they once misused their bodies. They may reject themselves because they were once rejected by someone else. Sometimes people are aware of their self-hatred and self-rejection, but sometimes they are quite unaware of the cause of their sexual difficulties because they have repressed their feelings below the level of consciousness. Conscious, half-conscious and subconscious feelings of self-rejection may ultimately lead to sexual impotence. Often, however, such negative attitudes have slightly less devastating consequences. Some men, for instance, may experience relative or intermittent failure to achieve sufficient erection to have complete sexual intercourse, or they may find themselves able to penetrate but not ejaculate. Some men may suffer from premature ejaculation. Women may discover themselves to be unable to reach a sexual climax, even with people whom they find attractive, or they may take an unusually long time to reach orgasm on occasion.

These difficulties may be more or less severe at different times of people's lives and with different partners, but they always cause a great deal of suffering. Moreover, because of the nature of human sexual intercourse, such sexual dysfunctions are never experienced in isolation. The sexual partner's anxieties about his or her own sexual inadequacies invariably add to the client's anxieties, and may even result in a client's coming to believe that he or she is being rejected by the desired sexual partner. That belief may represent an underlying truth about the instability of a particular sexual relationship, but it may equally well be a tragic misunderstanding of the feelings and difficulties experienced by the client's partner.

People who are afraid of being rejected often invite rejection. Their approach to other people can be awkward. They may anticipate rejection by retreating from a relationship before it has really become established. They do this because consciously or subconsciously they feel so unworthy of love that they cannot believe that another person could come to love them even though the signs of love may be obvious to outside observers. Even if they persevere with the relationship to the point where sexual intercourse becomes possible they may withdraw from full union at the last possible minute rather than risk the pain of exposing their own love and need for love.

Predictably, the roots of this kind of avoidance behaviour often lie in childhood. Children who are unwanted and unloved, or those who have once known some love and then had that love withdrawn, often grow up with a lively fear of rejection because of the terrible pain it caused them during their formative years. They do not allow themselves to love because they know that to do so may lead to worse pain that that of remaining unloved and sexually unfulfilled. In their circumstances sexual inadequacy can be a defence mechanism for the protection of their inner selves.

Fear, conscious or subconscious, self-rejection and real rejection by other people, account for many people's failures to achieve satisfactory sexual intercourse. Other possible causes of inadequacy range from adolescent sexual experiments of which clients are subsequently ashamed to resentment against the sexual partner for some real or imagined sexual cruelty or infidelity. Sometimes the cause of the inadequacy can be found quite easily through careful history-taking, but at other times the cause is much more elusive. Clients are often helped by knowing some of the reasons which have contributed to their difficulties, but happily the successful treatment of many of these conditions is not dependent upon the precise diagnosis of their origins. Some of these treatments will be discussed in the chapter on sexual therapy. Here it is sufficient to say that a combination of behaviour therapy and frank discussion is often very effective, and a great many people who suffer from various forms of sexual inadequacy can be helped if only they can be persuaded to seek help.

Those who suffer from sexual inadequacy need sympathy and help from those who are close to them. They often receive a lot of emotional support from their sexual partners who co-operate readily with therapists. Counsellors and psychiatrists likewise can do a great deal to help and their efforts are often very effective. However, sexual partners and counsellors alike do not usually find it nearly so easy to help individuals who are disgruntled or unhappy with their sexual partners.

Sexual disharmony

People who have happy and straightforward sexual relationships have no need of sexual counsellors. Those who do need sexual counselling often present their counsellors with incredibly complicated stories which reveal the chaotic and tangled nature of their relationships.

Unhappy sexual relationships are common. Each problem relationship has its own pattern so that no two case histories are ever identical; yet the following one shows some features which are typical of many of the life stories of clients who initially seek help because of unsatisfactory sexual relationships. Their sexual problems often point to a deeper malaise in their inter-personal relationships.

Geoffrey and Hannah were Roman Catholics. They had five children. Although Hannah never enjoyed sexual intercourse very much she never refused Geoffrey's advances because she regarded sexual intercourse as his right and her duty. After the fifth child, however, her doctor warned her that another pregnancy might gravely impair her health and ability to care for her family. He offered her contraceptive advice, but Hannah did not feel able to break the rules of her Church which forbade artificial methods of birth control.

After this, Hannah's attitude towards sexual intercourse changed. She was afraid of another pregnancy, so she began to feel afraid of sexual intercourse and she avoided it whenever she could. Then she began to criticize Geoffrey for his apparent lack of self-control. She noticed things about his appearance and sexual behaviour which she had not seen before and which she disliked increasingly as time went by. She made her disgust apparent. Geoffrey was much upset. He disliked imposing himself on his wife; yet he knew that his sexual needs were insistent. Neither his doctor nor his priest seemed to understand his feelings at all.

Hannah and Geoffrey began to quarrel more frequently and openly than they had done during the first decade of their marriage. Their children were drawn into the conflict and found themselves forced to take sides. Hannah felt guilty about her feelings towards her husband, but she persuaded herself that her husband merely wanted to make selfish use of her body and that he did not really love her and his children. Geoffrey began to come home late. He often went out alone in order to avoid the constant rows at home. At first he filled his time with work. Then he began to go out with other women. Eventually he found himself someone who could act as a replacement for Hannah and who had no scruples about enjoying sexual intercourse. When Geoffrey and Hannah's youngest child was two years old he deserted his family, and went to live with Amy.

Geoffrey set up home with his new partner and had a child by her before he discovered how much he yearned for his first family. During the first year of his absence Hannah was left on her own, nursing her bitter feelings of loneliness and jealousy.

But she was determined not to let her feelings rule her life. She knew that she was partially to blame for the marital breakdown, yet she did not believe the marriage was over. She decided not to reproach Geoffrey for his irresponsibility, nor to ask for a divorce. Instead, she encouraged him to visit her and the children as often as possible. At this stage she began to see a counsellor to try to get herself and her sexual problems into perspective. She needed to share her bitter feelings with someone else and to discuss her plans for the future with an impartial adviser. Fortunately for her, her relationship with Geoffrey improved. By the end of the third year of separation Geoffrey was spending every other weekend at home. By the fourth year he had returned home to live and was visiting his other family one night a week and every other weekend.

None of this happened without painful suffering. Geoffrey, Hannah, Amy and their children all went through considerable pain before they reached their compromise decision. Hannah decided that her conscience must allow her to use birth control. This change of heart enabled her and Geoffrey to rediscover each other as lovers but caused unhappiness to Amy. Geoffrey did not desert his mistress and child. Hannah did not ask him to do so, and Amy decided that she preferred to go on as they were rather than risk losing her lover altogether. Three people's lives had been permanently changed through one person's sexual problem, but all three thought that their compromise was a responsible way of behaving under their own particular circumstances.

The counsellor who listened to Hannah throughout her four long years of sexual frustration, loneliness and self-reproach often wondered whether Hannah's suffering would end in happiness. She knew that Geoffrey and Hannah might develop fixed attitudes of rejection of each other at any time. She could only try to keep the lines of communication open between them, and hope that any love for each other which might remain could begin to grow again as they came together to discuss and work for their children's welfare. At first, she had no direct access to either Geoffrey or Amy, although later they did make some contact with her at a time when Amy was feeling very miserable because of her inability to win Geoffrey's whole-hearted love.

The counsellor's role in this instance was primarily that of a concerned listener. She was, nevertheless, aware that she was not impartial. She knew that her sympathies lay more with Hannah

59

and her children than with Geoffrey and Amy and her baby. She found herself encouraging Hannah to persevere with her refusal to give Geoffrey a civil divorce so that he could remarry. The counsellor made allowances for her bias in favour of Hannah yet she knew that her empathy with her client influenced the eventual outcome of the case.

This case history illustrates some of the difficulties which confront those who undertake marital or sexual counselling. To begin with, the interactions between sexual partners who are unhappy because of sexual disharmony are nearly always more complex than they appear to be on first acquaintance. Then, a couple's problems may often involve other people to whom the counsellors seldom have direct access unless they happen to work in a family therapy unit which can deal with parents and children as an entity. In addition the person who is most obviously distressed is not always the one who needs the greatest amount of outside help. Finally, although counsellors are initially welcome as helpful outsiders they, too, become part of the problem since their intervention in the unhappy relationships of their clients creates its own dynamic for better or worse.

The way in which counsellors can use their interventionist role creatively is discussed in more detail in a later chapter. It is mentioned here because clients' expectations of their counsellors are so important. The counsellors' responses to those expectations may well determine the future happiness or unhappiness of their clients, as Andrew's story demonstrates.

Andrew came to the counsellor on his own initiative and he came alone. He was married to Selina who was two years younger than himself. The couple's sexual relationship had never been very satisfactory, even at the time of their marriage fifteen years previously. Andrew had always supposed that he was undersexed. He was glad that Selina did not make excessive sexual demands on him. They shared their love of their home and had many other interests in common. They thought of themselves as great friends who were happily married. In time they had two children both of whom were conceived during idyllic summer holidays in Greece. Andrew was devoted to his children. He and Selina settled into comfortable domesticity. So it was a considerable shock to him when he fell in love with Michael who had come to work at the same firm.

At first Andrew resisted this new and overwhelming passion, but within a few months they were lovers. Selina sensed the difference in her husband. She thought that he was in love with another woman and was deeply affronted when she accidentally discovered that her rival was another man. She presented Andrew with an ultimatum which left him little room for manoeuvre. His love for his children overrode his desire for Michael.

Andrew, Selina and their two children uprooted themselves from the neighbourhood where they had lived all their married life and moved to another part of the country to begin life afresh. Unfortunately, Selina disliked her new home and neighbourhood and did not find it easy to make new friends. She continued to be suspicious whenever Andrew came home late. She criticized him unmercifully, especially when he did not defend himself against her verbal abuse. Andrew became totally impotent with her but found that he was still tormented by memories of his relationship with Michael.

Andrew's distress over his impotence was so obvious that after a while Selina demanded that he should go to the doctor to see if he could be 'cured' of his homosexual inclinations. When the consultations began Andrew seemed quite eager to undergo any treatment that would help him to stay with his wife and family. However, the counsellor could not persuade him to let her see his wife. Andrew also told her that Michael lived too far away to come; he implied that it would be useless to involve an 'ex-boy friend' in his present problems. As the therapy sessions proceeded it became quite evident that Andrew was using them to delay facing his conflict. He was a skilled manipulator, even though he was partially unaware of what he was doing, and he relied on the counsellor's preference for a non-directive approach in order to postpone a decision indefinitely. For a time the counsellor did not see what was happening but eventually she understood that she was being sucked into a collusive relationship which was going to be therapeutically sterile. So she altered the dynamics of the relationship by using tactics which forced Andrew to realize exactly what he might do to his wife and children if he stayed with them without being able to commit himself whole-heartedly to Selina.

A week later Andrew left home and went to live with Michael. Selina eventually remarried. The children grew up into relatively healthy adults. The counsellor felt guilty for a time because of her part in the marital break-up, although she realized that her counter-manipulation had been a necessary technique in this particular deadlocked situation in order to free all its victims from a prolonged period of unhappiness. In later years she learnt that all the people who had been caught up in the emotional struggle had come to feel that their short-term pain was vindicated by their ultimate happiness.

These illustrations of the way in which sexual disharmony and unhappiness can play havoc with people's lives have been chosen to illustrate particular aspects of the work of sexual counsellors. There are, of course, many other causes of sexual unhappiness than the ones cited here, and there are many different manifestations of disharmony which are not adequately covered. Nevertheless, these illustrations serve to point to the importance of the sexual drive in people's lives and to the vital necessity of taking an adequate history of the sexual relationships in clients' lives where sexual disharmony is a presenting symptom. They also show how the relationships between clients and counsellors can affect the lives of those involved.

It is impossible to design textbook solutions which can be applied to every conflict where sexual disharmony is a symptom. Counsellors can learn to cope with most situations provided that they understand sexual behaviour, have a good working knowledge of commonly occurring sexual problems and can recognize the symptoms of sexual isolation, inadequacy and disharmony. Their work is made much easier if they are able to be frank and open minded in their discussion of people's sexual difficulties and are able to establish a good rapport with their clients. It is not enough, however, to be skilled, sympathetic and tolerant in this kind of work. Counsellors can bring all these qualities to their work and still fail their clients if they ignore the moral issues which underlie their clients' particular difficulties.

Clients sometimes complain that their counsellors give them advice which contradicts their own cherished moral beliefs. That may happen, for instance, when a practising Roman Catholic client meets a militantly atheistic counsellor, or vice versa, but such an outright clash of moral beliefs is not so very common in present-day practice because most counsellors are willing to avoid such head-on collisions with their clients. Some counsellors do this by trying to adopt a morally neutral stance towards all sexual problems. Such a non-moral attitude can be just as harmful to clients as a very dogmatic approach because the clients may not feel that they are talking to real people if they are allowed to talk only to opinionless counsellors on to whom they are permitted to project their own ideas and emotions. Counsellors who can retain their own moral opinions while respecting those of their clients can provide their clients with a moral framework against which they can test out their own ideas and feelings. If clients are allowed to do this they may be able to reach decisions which are right for them even though they may be wrong for the counsellor if she or he were in a similar situation.

Whenever clients come to counsellors they bring with them not only their immediate conflicts and difficulties but also themselves and their future expectations. They know that the moral decisions they make at crisis points in their lives will inevitably affect their future. These decisions are important. They are often difficult to make. That is why so many people who have sexual problems involving moral decisions turn to counsellors for help. This means that counsellors will spend a large proportion of their available consultation time with clients who have to make these kinds of decision. Many of these clients want to make moral choices which can help them to integrate their sexual needs and behaviour into their lives in such a way that they can become whole persons who can live in harmony with themselves and their chosen partners.

THREE
Some Moral Problems

It is not easy to define wholeness or health in positive terms. When people bring their problems to a counsellor or doctor they are sometimes asked what they expect to be the outcome of their counselling or treatment sessions. Many of them reply in somewhat negative terms. They may hope, for instance, for the removal of this or that physical pain, disability or emotional suffering. They often hope that their problem will disappear. Their ideas about well-being nearly always include an absence of any malaise.

A number of people will demand not only the removal of their suffering but also expect to return to the condition of health they enjoyed in their youth or thought they had prior to their illness. These rather negative expectations look backwards and ignore the potential of the future, although it should be obvious that once people have met with pain, illness, emotional suffering, or faced a personal crisis, they cannot again be the same people as they were before. The course of their lives may be permanently altered by the way they deal with their problems. Counsellors know all this, but even they may be rather hazy about their goals when they undertake a new relationship with a client. They may be content to comply with their client's requests and be satisfied if they can remove pain, ease suffering or solve a few practical problems. These are important interim goals, but counsellors who are content with these limited objectives will miss the more complete satisfaction that comes from helping people to search for their ultimate goal of wholeness or positive health.

Health and wholeness are words which are contrasted with those of illness and fragmentation, and because health

65

and illness are set in opposition to each other they also become invested with different values. So words like 'good' become attached to health, and 'bad' to illness.

'Good' and 'bad' may be used as descriptive terms. An individual might, for instance, think of sexual potency as 'good' because potency is thought of as healthy. Impotence could be thought of as 'bad' because it is felt to be a sign of illness. These terms can be used without assigning moral value to them, and without necessarily implying that it is always 'good' to be potent, and always 'bad' to be impotent.

'Good' and 'bad', however, are often used as words to which moral value is attached. Sexual continence is often thought of as 'good', for example, and promiscuity as 'bad', and this use of these particular words may sometimes contradict the ideas of 'good' and 'bad' which have been used to describe potency and impotency in another context. There may be occasions when an individual and the community may decide that impotence is 'good' if, for instance, it helps a sexual offender to refrain from criminal behaviour. In certain circumstances both the sexual offender and the community may come to think that chemical castration is 'good', or at least expedient for offender and community alike. This is an extreme example, but it shows that when descriptive words are used to convey value judgements they can be used in such a variety of ways that they do not convey their exact meaning unless they are understood to be used in a particular context.

The way in which these value-loaded words are used also depends on the particular point of view of the person who uses them as descriptive terms. If, for instance, the speaker's stance is absolutist[1] then one end of the good-bad scale is always closer to the ideal and must be labelled 'good' while the other pole is distant from the source of all good and must be thought of as 'bad'. So to the absolutist health and wholeness are always seen as good ends in themselves and the opposites are always seen as 'bad' or

66

'evil'. If the speaker is a relativist then 'good' and 'bad' are held to be relative concepts so that what is 'good' in one situation can be thought of as 'bad' in another.

Moral theologians tend to be absolutists, and situational ethicists are always relativists, but most people, counsellors and clients alike, are likely to find themselves bewildered from time to time by these very different ways of looking at the concepts of 'good' and 'bad', especially where these terms are used to describe moral 'good' and 'evil'. So they often swing uneasily between absolutism and relativism, often without noticing which stance they have adopted in particular circumstances.

The point of drawing attention to these various ways of looking at 'good' and 'evil' is that people's moral attitudes accompany them wherever they go, so they are brought into the counsellor's presence along with the more immediate problem which the client wishes to discuss. The client's ethical and religious beliefs invariably interact with the counsellor's own beliefs and form an important part of their relationship even though neither of them may refer to those underlying beliefs openly. They are therefore important to the therapeutic relationship and can be understood to be potential assets or liabilities in any dialogue about sexual problems.

Sexual ethics is the philosophy or code distinguishing the 'good' and the 'bad' in human sexual conduct.[2] Sexual ethics embraces many aspects of personal behaviour and extends to a wide range of social issues like contraception, abortion, sterilization, artificial insemination and surrogate sex therapy.

Counsellors need to work with their clients' value-systems as far as possible, although there will always be occasions when in conscience they cannot agree with their clients, and they will sometimes have to separate from them because of this disagreement. They should not, however, assume that 'the customer is always right', for the client may be working with a value-system which is

67

distorted by illness or by the problem itself, or which the client has adopted for convenience but which really goes against her or his conscience. Moreover, if counsellors take their clients' problems seriously there will be occasions on which they will feel it right to remind them that there are other solutions besides the ones which the clients appear to prefer. They will try to help them to consider all the other possibilities realistically, having regard to the clients' future needs as well as their present ones.

Although this seems to be a sensible way of using a counsellors' skills and experience, clients do not always find it pleasant to be reminded of other choices which they have already considered and rejected, or are determined not to think about. Counsellors are likely to find themselves involved in consultations which are marked by emotional reactions over the moral aspects of the problem. This kind of situation often arises, for instance, over pre-marital sex.

Pre-marital Sex

Linda was just sixteen when her mother brought her to the doctor.

'It's time she went on the "pill",' she said. 'Linda can't be trusted to behave herself, now she's got a boy friend. They're off to Spain for a holiday next month. I'd prefer her to go on the pill than get pregnant.'

Linda nodded. 'It's ok, isn't it?' she said. 'I mean, you hear things about the pill.'

The doctor was busy. He answered Linda's anxiety about the side-effects of oral contraceptives, asked her some questions about her health and menstrual cycle, took her blood pressure and wrote the prescription for a three-month supply of a low-dose pill.

The consultation was over in five minutes.

This story is unusual only in that Linda's mother had accompanied her to the doctor. Most young women over the age of legal consent, and a few who are not, will come to a clinic on their own. Had Linda done so the doctor might have discussed the matter with her in more detail. Even so, their conversation might have been confined to the practical short- and long-term physical and psychological consequences of early sexual intercourse. Many clients and doctors would consider it inappropriate to discuss the moral aspects of pre-marital sex in the context of a consultation about birth control. Yet, in the author's experience many people do want to discuss the rights and wrongs of their proposed actions and actual behaviour with counsellors who are willing to listen and exchange views.

Moral attitudes towards pre-marital sex have undergone considerable change since the advent of reliable methods of birth control. Most people used to think that men could engage in sexual intercourse without deep emotional involvement whereas women had a deeper emotional investment in sexual intercourse because they saw it as part of home-making and 'nesting'. This difference in women's and men's attitudes towards sexual intercourse is still apparent in some people, especially older and religious people, but women's attitudes towards pre-marital sexual relationships have undergone rapid and radical changes since their emancipation from the fear of conceiving unexpected or unwanted children. Many women now enjoy sexual intercourse as a physical activity. They are able to fall in love without expecting the relationship to be permanent or connecting it with home-making or childbearing.

On the other hand some women and men agree to refrain from sexual intercourse at an early state of their relationship because they do not want to engage in sexual intimacy until they are seriously considering marriage. Many people, possibly the majority, want to have sexual intercourse with the person they love only when they are committed to each other in a loving relationship which has some hope of permanence in it.

The existence of these changing attitudes towards pre-marital sex in a large number of people means that the social reasons against pre-marital sexual intercourse are shifting away from fears about its consequences towards an insistence on its being an expression of committed love. Present and future moral attitudes towards sexual intercourse are, therefore, likely to be based increasingly upon a love ethic rather than one of fear.

Those who look at pre-marital sexual intercourse from a point of view which is based upon love ethics know that pre-marital chastity which is undertaken for the sake of love is different from continence, which is the product of fear. They know that loving pre-marital chastity can lay the foundations of a happy and successful marriage and they can support couples who choose this expression of commitment to each other. On the other hand, they might also feel that it might be right for two people who love each other to express their love through sexual intercourse under certain circumstances. An engaged couple, for instance, may decide to postpone marriage until they had enough money to buy a home and start a family but agree to live together in token of their commitment to each other for life. A women and man waiting for a divorce to come through might decide that their particular circumstances warranted their engaging in pre-marital intercourse.

Counsellors who work with people who are struggling to make the right decisions about pre-marital intercourse will find themselves confronted with a wide range of attitudes towards sexual intercourse before marriage. In principle either they or their clients might be absolutist or relativist, but in practice their feelings, as well as those of their clients, are less likely to be outraged when the couple concerned are young, engaged and free from other obligations, and more likely to feel affronted when one of the couple is already married or committed to another person. In those circumstances pre-marital sexual intercourse may also be extra-marital sexual intercourse and this fact complicates the issues.

Extra-marital sex

Social fears about pre-marital sexual intercourse may have diminished in recent years but fears about extra-marital sexual relationships have been increased by the rapidly rising rate of divorce in western countries. At least one in four marriages can expect to end in the divorce courts in most European communities and one in three will end in the same way in the United States of America.

Adultery remains one of the major causes of marital unhappiness, since the abandoned partner often feels deeply rejected by the unfaithful partner. Counsellors who have to deal with marital infidelity need much patience if they are to enable unhappy people to find their own solutions to particular problems. People need more time than they often think at the beginning of their trials if they are to find creative solutions to their special problems. One of the responsibilities of a counsellor is that of trying to prevent the disputants from taking any precipitate action which they might later regret. Sheila's case history illustrates how difficult it can be for everyone concerned to exercise this kind of patience.

Sheila was a devout Methodist married to an Anglican business man called Robert. They had one daughter, Ann. When Ann was ten years old Sheila decided to return to work. She took a short refresher course and obtained a good post as a private secretary. A year later she discovered that she was in love with her bachelor employer and he with her.

Sheila knew that she still loved her husband and child so she left her work and John. She tried to settle down at home, but she could not coerce her heart to follow her head; so she began a clandestine existence. She and John found ways of meeting in secret once or twice a week, when her husband was at work and her child at school or with friends. When she was with John she felt guilty about Robert, but when she went home to Robert she found that she missed John. The strain on her face betrayed her. When Robert discovered her secret there was a row, then another, then a third. All three of them became miserable.

Sheila could not decide between her two men. Both of them in turn tried leaving her, but neither succeeded in doing so for more than a few weeks. Sheila became depressed and went to a marriage guidance counsellor. Six months later, however, the situation had not changed very much. Sheila would talk about leaving home or leaving John, but did neither. She had lost weight. She slept poorly, wept a good deal and felt tired most of the time. She still managed to care adequately for her home and daughter who now called John 'uncle' and seemed happy in his company.

The counsellor who had started the case with optimism now felt impatient whenever Sheila came to see her. She had become a professional counsellor after her own divorce. She had always been proud that she had ended her own marriage without any rancour so that she and her husband had remained good friends. She now felt herself to be an accessory to Sheila's manipulative behaviour. On several occasions she felt so defeated by Sheila's indecision and her male partners' collusive behaviour that she suggested that they stop their fruitless consultations but Sheila begged for them to go on and so she continued to work with her without much hope.

After two years of stalemate Sheila came to tell the counsellor that the three of them had decided to live together. The counsellor was horrified and foresaw all kinds of difficulties ahead of them. Her own attempts to tolerate her husband's mistresses had ended in failure and she felt that Robert's jealousy and Ann's bewilderment would make it impossible for three adults and a 'teenager' to live together. She told Sheila that she must do whatever she genuinely felt to be for the best, but that as a counsellor she could not feel happy about such an unorthodox experiment. She added that she could not see how devout Christians like Sheila, Robert and John could contemplate such a relationship and remain Christians. On that tense note she and Sheila parted company.

Three years later the counsellor met Sheila again and learnt that they were all still living happily together although the experiment had not been without its problems.

This case history illustrates some of the difficulties which face counsellors when they work with people rather than textbook cases. People do not always do what they ought to do. They sometimes take an inordinate amount of time making up their minds about what they want to do. They make choices which appear to be foolhardy. They confound their critics by making a success of an impossible situation: or sometimes they fail.

In this particular case it would be easy to say that the best solution would have been for Sheila to leave her lover and return to her husband. At one time the counsellor thought that this would happen, but in the event her opinion was challenged by her client's decision. The counsellor's reactions to this trio's solution to their problem is not at all unusual, for many who are involved in other people's conflicts are disturbed by echoes of these conflicts in their own lives. They may feel very unhappy, even guilty, about their own role in such conflicts, especially where the problems are unusual, the conflicts prolonged and the solutions unorthodox. Many counsellors learn to tolerate their own resurgent emotions and guilt feelings. Some are helped by discussing their reactions to problem situations with colleagues or in a therapeutic group of their own. Christians who engage in this kind of work have special problems of conscience, especially when their principles are threatened by pragmatic considerations. An experienced priest, lay person, or group of fellow-Christians can provide invaluable support to counsellors who find themselves in ethical difficulties. Open discussion can often clarify their dilemma even if it cannot be resolved, and the relief of being able to face their internal conflict with colleagues who can share their distress without being unduly upset by it is considerable.

Individual attitudes towards extra-marital sexual intercourse depend to a large extent upon personal experience and the attitudes and experience of close relatives and friends, but the social climate of the day also exerts its influence on people's moral attitudes. Oscar Wilde's statement, 'Modern morality consists in accepting the standards of one's own age',[3] may represent a cynical view of the way in which moral values are acquired, but it has relevance in a society which is struggling to readjust itself from a fear ethic to a love ethic, since many people find themselves confused and uncertain about the nature of their moral standards. The old standard of 'thou shalt not' has been partially abandoned but it has not yet been replaced by the more positive ethic of 'thou shalt'. This means that during the transition period there appear to be no moral standards which will command universal acceptance.

There is some evidence to suggest that many men and women in society now expect the same standards of morality in both partners to a marriage. They either expect both partners to be faithful to their marriage vows, or they consider that both partners should be able to enjoy extra-marital sexual relationships without necessarily feeling that their marriage is threatened thereby.

Adultery is not the only extra-marital relationship which interferes with marriages. Any sexual relationship between one partner to a marriage and someone else of the same sex can affect the stability of a marriage in much the same way as adultery. Some people are unable to accept their partner's homosexual relationships. Others can tolerate them quite easily.

People often ask whether homosexual unions are similar to or different from heterosexual experience in marriage. Present evidence cannot give a definitive answer to this question. It is certain, however, that the pain and suffering caused by sexual infidelity is as real for homosexuals as for heterosexuals. In this respect homosexuals and heterosexuals share a human experience, and they appear to react to it in similar ways. Sexual infidelity between homosexuals is not, therefore, treated seperately.

All counsellors know that there will be many occasions on which they will have to share their client's failure to resolve a sexual problem. Unfortunately, in western society a great many people have to face the problem of what they should do when their love for their partner is dead, or when their own love is rejected by a partner who once loved them.

Death of sexual relationships

Judging by the rising divorce statistics and the breakdown rate in contractual agreements between unmarried people, most men and women now accept that it is useless for two people to try to live together when all love between them is dead. Nevertheless divorce or separation remains a tragedy and a major cause of psychological distress and disorder.

When two people begin to consider divorce or separation as a possible solution to their problems they face a difficult task. They have to think about their relationship in an atmosphere which is charged with strong emotions. The couple may discuss their affairs coolly and rationally on one occasion so that they can draw up sensible plans for their own and their dependants' future lives. Within hours or days, all these plans may be overturned because of a sudden upsurge of emotion. Sometimes powerful feelings of optimism can destroy a person's ability to make a rational decision about leaving home. At other times destructive emotions, like jealousy and the desire for revenge, can end a relationship which once looked viable. It is, therefore, important for two people who are thinking of divorce or separation to be able to look at their relationship from many different angles and to take their time about it.

Counsellors can be very helpful during this difficult time when hard decisions have to be made. The counsellor's main task is to listen to what is said, to note what is not said, to explore what is hidden or ignored and to try to uncover any signs of life in the relationship which suggest that the couple could stay together. The following two case histories show how one relationship seemed doomed to death, but eventually survived, while the other died in

75

spite of the partners' strenuous efforts to keep it alive.

Jennifer came to the counsellor by herself. She said that she knew that David would never come with her so she had not asked him to do so. According to her, their marriage was in difficulties because of David's attitude to her role as his wife.

She was certain that their problems could be solved if only David would stop treating her as a servant.

'He's just a spoilt child,' she said. 'His mother treated him as if he were a little god. She waited on him hand and foot and gave him whatever he wanted. He never helped in the house when he was a boy and he won't do anything to help me now. He says that housework is women's work. He gives me the housekeeping money and spends only a little of his own money down at the pub or watching football. He saves the rest and says that we can't even afford to go out now as we did when we were courting. I'm bored, fed up and frustrated. I'm just a shut-in drudge and a convenient sex-object. I might as well be a housekeeper or a prostitute except that David doesn't have to pay out as much for me as he would have to for either of them.'

During the first consultation it was evident that Jennifer had plenty of grievances. She poured out her complaints in a whining voice. After a while the counsellor asked her to list some of David's assets. The tone of Jennifer's voice changed. She insisted that sexual intercourse with David was 'marvellous'. She added that he was a good father, a kind husband; a clean-living man, a hard worker. She was convinced that he only had to change his attitude towards her 'just a little' and they would be 'happy ever after'.

Asked about her own assets, Jennifer sighed. She said that David always praised her cooking. He thought she was a good mother. He was proud of her beauty. She was 'good in bed'. 'Well,' said the counsellor, 'that's quite a list. What doesn't he like about you, then?'

'Oh, I'm untidy,' Jennifer replied. 'I'm lazy, too, given half a chance. And I spend money like water when I've got it. He's always nagging me about that. But, I think he expects me to be too perfect, and to work too hard.' Her voice became angry. 'He says I'm extravagant. I think he's mean.'

During the next few sessions with the counsellor Jennifer continued to complain about David's treatment of her. She showed remarkably little insight into her own behaviour and the way in which it might have reinforced David's attitudes. She wanted David to treat her as an adult, yet much of her behaviour encouraged him to think of her as an irresponsible child. She accused him of meanness, yet she admitted that she 'spent money like water' whenever she had the chance. She wanted David to change, yet failed to see that he might only be able to change if she grew up.

The counsellor thought that the marriage had no chance of surviving unless the couple's conflict over money could be solved. Yet, for a long time Jennifer kept on grumbling about David and ignoring her own faults. Then the day came when the counsellor could stand it no longer. She told Jennifer how irritating her continual petulence and self-justification was. By that time their relationship was good enough for Jennifer to accept this display of anger from her counsellor, who was then able to help her client to see herself in a more realistic way.

This session proved to be a turning point. Some weeks later Jennifer came to the counsellor in a happier mood. She said that she and David had struck a bargain. The occasion was a fierce argument during which David had accused her of wasting their money on an expensive dress. Instead of turning her back on him or taunting him with his meanness as she usually did, Jennifer agreed with him. She offered to give up some of her extravagances if David would agree to put the money they saved in this way towards a new family car. David was astonished. He agreed to her plan although he had previously said they could not afford a new car, despite a reasonable bank balance. He did not think Jennifer would be able to control her impulsive spending. But he was wrong. Jennifer stopped being so extravagant. David learnt to be more generous. As the result of their joint endeavour the marriage began to flourish and grow.

This marriage was almost dead when it was revived because Jennifer gained enough insight into her own distorted thinking to be able to react to a familiar quarrel in an entirely new way. Unfortunately the outcome is not always so happy. In a similar case another client, Susan, thought that her marriage was alive when it was dead.

Like Jennifer, Susan was extravagant and her husband, Mark, had done his best to restrict her spending sprees. They quarrelled about money incessantly until Susan decided to solve her problem by getting another man to pay some of her bills. She and Mark had agreed that each of them should be free to make sexual relationships outside the marriage, and from time to time both of them had enjoyed transient affairs without allowing their joint happiness to be undermined. So this time Susan found herself a rich man who could easily afford to pay for some of her pleasures. She thought that Mark would be pleased to see that their joint bank account was no longer overdrawn, and was genuinely surprised when he took her to task for accepting money from another man. She returned his anger with interest because she knew that he sometimes accepted expensive presents from his lady friends. Their anger with each other became divisive and disruptive.

Each began to criticize the other in ways previously alien to both. When they realized this they tried to put things right. Susan broke off her 'affair'. They tried having separate bank accounts. Susan even managed to save some money. They thought that sexual fidelity might help them to stay together. For a time they continued to pretend that their continuing sexual compatibility could cement their relationship. Both tried hard, but their determination to avoid arguments damaged their relationship more than their anger with each other had done. The day came when Mark announced that Susan's behaviour no longer pleased or displeased him. She merely bored him. Susan could not accept the reality of this disastrous sign of the impending death of a relationship. She continued to try to mend the marriage, but within two months of that statement Mark was gone. Susan then came to a counsellor in a state of shocked grief. She was still unable to take in the full implication of Mark's indifference to her. She needed many months of counselling before she could come to terms with the truth that her marriage was over.

These two accounts of unhappy marriages point to some signs which can indicate whether or not a partnership which has run into trouble is viable. Such a relationship can be presumed to be alive if the partners still care about each other despite their dissensions. People can hurt and even damage each other and still remain united provided that their quarrels can ultimately lead to a growth in their understanding and love for each other, and provided that they can find areas of mutual interest and harmony in

78

their lives. By way of contrast a sexual relationship can be assumed to be moribund if one partner becomes totally indifferent to the other's needs and sufferings, if the attitudes of either remain so fixed that she or he cannot change, or if they cannot find significant areas of interest to share.

It is probably unsafe to rely on only one or two signs of impending death as an absolute indication that a particular relationship is in a terminal phase, because it is true that relationships which seem to be terminal have been known to survive despite all expectations. When people realize that a once-precious relationship is dead, they have to decide what to do about their situation.

Some people have no difficulty. They translate reality into divorce, legal or permanent separation. They go through the necessary formalities quite stoically and emerge the other side as individuals who feel free to make new relationships. Many people who discover that their marriage or partnership relationship is dead need to mourn its passing for quite a while before they can bring themselves to acknowledge that fact openly. Others cling to each other long after their relationship is dead, either because they need the security offered by their formal status or because it is convenient to both of them to live in the same house.

Religious people who are considering divorce sometimes have added burdens to bear since their individual needs do not always fit into a pattern which is acceptable to the official teaching of their Church or faith. These religious attitudes towards the severance of marital ties and the remarriage of divorcees do affect personal decisions and sometimes add to the difficulties of making the best possible choice. It is rare today to find people who make conformity to their Church's ruling the sole reason for their decision to remain married when the relationship between them and their partners has died.

When marriages and established partnerships die the

partners may never see each other again. If that happens they may pass through a period of grieving which is akin to that of the widow or widower. More often, however, the former partners retain a financial link through the payment of alimony or child-maintenance allowance, and sometimes they share a common task through the care and upbringing of their children. Nevertheless, there has been 'a death in the family' and the post-mortem relationships can produce problems which are somewhat similar to those which can beset some people after the physical death of their partners.

Life after the death of sexual relationships

It is well known that bereavement is a traumatic event for the surviving partner. In an important book on *The Dying Patient*, edited by Ronald W. Raven, J. R. Casswell comments:

It is perhaps, most helpful to regard bereavement as an amputation. It is a trauma in the realm of the affections and emotions analagous to the loss of a limb in the physical realm, in fact to the loss of more than a limb. Catullus wrote of the lady of his affections as 'the half of my life', and many a husband and wife have felt that more than half a life has been taken when the other partner has been removed by death.[4]

Those who survive the death of their partner become accident prone and vulnerable to illness during the first two years after their bereavement, and there is an increased mortality and morbidity among widows and widowers during that period. People who are divorced or separated suffer in much the same way. They share many of the same problems as those who are bereft of their partners by physical death. They may have to face financial hardship. They sometimes have to move away from cherished homes. They may be left with young children to bring up on their own. They may have to go out to work for the first time in many years. They have to get on with living when they are lonely, grieving for the past and often afraid for the future. It is not surprising that in these circumstances many people become ill or make mistakes of judgement and find themselves in all kinds of difficulties.

The immediate period of bereavement is characterized by numbness, amounting sometimes to disbelief. When that phase has passed it is followed by a longer period of bitter mourning during which the past relationship is seen unrealistically because the grieving mind blots out all the bad things that happened and tends to idealize the former partner or relationship. Some people find that the memories which surround them in their home are so painful that they will make precipitate decisions. They will, for instance, decide to move away from their neighbourhood and friends. They may sell their homes and possessions cheaply, well below the market price. They may destroy letters and burn clothes and even photographs in order to escape their painful memories, and their actions are often deeply regretted at a later date.

Recently bereaved people sometimes feel very angry with their former partners or other people who they feel have been responsible for their present suffering. A widowed spouse may, for instance, blame the dead partner for not going to the doctor at an early stage of the fatal illness. Bereaved families sometimes unjustly accuse medical attendants of negligence. Some people who are going through divorce put all the blame for the breakdown of their marriage on to their ex-partner. They may sue for huge and unrealistic sums of alimony, or become involved in prolonged legal battles over the custody of the children. Other people turn their anger in on themselves. They blame themselves for the death of their spouse, close relative or relationship. They punish themselves in various ways. They may, for instance, eat less than enough to keep themselves healthy, refuse to go out, deny themselves company or any pleasure and feel obliged to go on mourning longer than is necessary.

During this bitter phase of mourning bereaved people need the company of close relatives, friends or counsellors who can take a more realistic view of their past relationship and of the circumstances surrounding the death of the former partner or sexual partnership. Bereaved people are often aware that they are living in an unreal world. They are grateful for the opportunity of measuring their fantasies against an outside opinion. They sometimes rely on trusted outsiders to keep them in touch with reality and to protect them from excessive withdrawal or precipitate reaction to the strong emotions which dominate their lives.

If all goes well, this time of mourning gives way gradually to the admission that one phase of life is over and another begun. People who are emerging from their grief find that they become able to enjoy past memories without retreating into them, and they begin to build the future in separation from the dead person or relationship, whether or not they again form close sexual relationships.

Sometimes, however, all does not go well. Excessive and prolonged grieving is a well-known hazard of bereavement. People who continue to be submerged in grief for their dead partners or relationships for more than two years often need more than a counsellor's support and encouragement if they are to be helped to recovery. Their grief has become pathological and their depression may yield only to drug or other therapy.

Some people do not grieve properly. They cannot face the pain so they deny it access to their conscious minds at an earlier stage than they should. When this happens the bereaved people may appear to be coping with their loss remarkably well. The grief may catch up with them only at a later date, and it may overtake them in a dramatic way as Lisa's story shows.

Lisa was forty-four years old when her husband left her. She and her teenage daughters had a secure council tenancy and an allowance from her ex-husband. Before and immediately after the divorce, Lisa had felt rejected and hurt. But she was determined to get on with life. Within a few months of her divorce she succeeded in captivating the attention of a rich widower. Ignoring her children's protests, and her friends' advice she married her new-found partner after having known him for only nine weeks. She gave up her own home and relinquished her alimony.

Within two weeks of her marriage Lisa discovered that she had made a dreadful mistake. She and the children were trapped in a situation from which there was no immediate or obvious escape.

Lisa took a massive overdose of drugs and landed up in hospital in a state of profound depression from which it took her over a year to recover. She was fortunate to be alive, although it took her many months to feel grateful to the friends who had saved her life.

Lisa's story is only one example of the way in which people can react precipitately to the pain of bereavement. Similar, though less dramatic, reactions are not uncommon. Counsellors are often invited to help people to cope with the consequences of their errors of judgement during the early stages of bereavement. Happily, many clients do recover. Some of them, however, have to learn to live with permanent disabilities.

So far, bereavement has been considered in the context of physical death and divorce or separation from a former sexual partner. But there are other less obvious deaths which occur during life. Many of these 'mini-deaths' occur through illness. A woman, for instance, may feel a deep sense of loss after the amputation of a breast or after a hysterectomy. A man may grieve if he is found to be sterile, or loses a testicle. These 'mini-deaths' are tragic. They leave permanent damage in people's lives. Other 'mini-deaths' occur in the lives of people who have been the victims of their own or other people's misuse of their human sexuality.

'Mini-deaths' which are the consequences of human actions seem even more tragic than the 'deaths' due to natural disaster because they might have been avoided. It is, for instance, impossible to obliterate the scars from the mind and body of a woman who has been disfigured with razor blades during a sexual orgy. It is sad to meet a young woman whose fertility has been wrecked by gonorrhea and who longs for the children she will never bear. It is difficult to speak confidently of future happiness to an adolescent girl who has been the victim of rape, or a boy who has been savagely assaulted by a man intent on buggery. It is very difficult to find any words which will comfort the parents of a child who has been sexually assaulted and then murdered.

Counsellors naturally shrink from involvement in these very destructive aspects of human sexuality. They prefer the relatively normal problems which occur when people live together. Counsellors cannot, however, escape the darker areas of human experience unless they deliberately select their cases and refuse to accept any client who is involved in sexual perversion, contacts venereal disease, asks for an abortion or sterilization, gets raped, or rapes. Some people do feel obliged in conscience to avoid this kind of counselling if it is likely to lead to their participation in a further destructive act, such as abortion or sterilization, but the majority of counsellors feel that they have a duty to tackle the unpleasant problems as well as the more rewarding ones, even though they know that they may have to share the responsibility of choosing the lesser of two evil solutions to a problem which has arisen directly from a destructive sexual act.

These destructive aspects of sexuality merit special consideration if counsellors are to be effective when they meet clients with certain particular problems.

FOUR
Destructive Sex

This chapter does not include any individual case histories. The reason for this deliberate omission is rather sad. It is that destructive sex unfortunately makes the headlines every day. The media thrive on stories about the many ways in which human beings can misuse their sexuality. Counsellors and clients are used to reading about sexual exploitation, sexual cruelty and sexual crimes in their daily newspapers, or they hear about these things on radio or television. It is, therefore, all too easy to find real-life case histories to illustrate the destructive aspects of human sexuality which are described in this chapter.

All human sexuality can be used destructively. Sex is a source of intense pleasure and as such it is open to the abuses of over-indulgence or extreme self-denial. Human beings degrade their humanity if they use their sexual drives for their own self-gratification at the expense of other people's needs. They distort their humanity if they repress or suppress their sexuality in such a way that it forces them to behave in unpleasant and uncontrollable ways. People who repress their sexuality are sometimes unaware of its effects on their lives although many other people can see what is happening to them.

It is known that certain genetic factors can affect the sexual behaviour of individuals. That fact is undeniable; yet, sex, being an instrument of love is also rooted in childhood experiences of loving and being loved, and so the roots of normal and abnormal sexual behaviour often lie in childhood relationships. It is often very difficult to know why it is that some children can develop into adults able to use their sexuality creatively for their own and other people's happiness while other children with similar backgrounds grow up into adults who use their sexuality selfishly and destructively. Yet, some experts feel fairly certain that they do understand some of the childhood experiences which contribute to adult difficulties. Dr Anthony Storr voices the conclusions of many counsellors in one of his books:

In dealing with adult neurotic problems, one is more and more forced to the conclusions that isolation, and an inability to mix with contemporaries at an early stage in childhood, are important determinants of adult difficulties.[1]

He goes on to discuss the way in which children learn to control their aggressive impulses, and he then turns to their sexual drives and says:

Similarly, isolated children grow up with little knowledge of sex. In the absence of games with contemporaries, their knowledge of their own sexuality and that of the opposite sex remains deficient. Children, if left to themselves, will explore each other's anatomy and play games which are imitations of adult sexual behaviour. They will also explore their own anatomy and discover that pleasure is to be obtained from their own genitals. Analysts know that the child who has never masturbated, and who cannot recall any childhood genital touching, is severely inhibited sexually, and less likely to be able to make a satisfactory adult sexual relationship.[2]

Isolation which persists into adult life sometimes finds its expression through the development of passionate attachments to non-human objects.

Bestiality and fetishism

The isolated individual may find real human beings too frightening to approach and then discover that it is easier to feel sexually roused by an animal or object than by another human being. Adults who have not been allowed to enjoy their sexuality as children sometimes find that they do not know or understand the various signals used by other men and women in sexual exchanges and foreplay because they have not had enough experience of sexual games during childhood to learn the basic art of sexual language and behaviour in social life. So they substitute animals or objects as sexual stimuli instead of women or fellow men.

Falling in love with animals, stuffed teddy bears or shiny boots is not necessarily destructive in itself. Many women and men become passionately attached to domestic pets, and many people are intrigued by the smell and feel of fur, cuddly toys, leather and other objects. The love of pets and aesthetic pleasure in objects of any kind can be creative since it can lead people to care deeply about the welfare of animals and the preservation of the objects they love. As with so many other aspects of sexuality, however, human beings can turn away from the loving desire to preserve and improve the objects of their affections, towards the desire to gratify themselves at all costs through the domination or possession of the desired objects. When they do that they misuse their own humanity. They can also misuse animals and things and destroy their intrinsic autonomy.

Bestiality is less common than fetishism, perhaps because the idea becomes repellent to many peple who allow themselves to imagine what it is like to have sexual intercourse with an animal. It is easy to understand in many ways because those who try it often say that it is possible to build a relationship between animals and human beings which is more real, loving and satisfying than anything they have experienced with their fellow-human beings.

Bestiality is condemned by some people because they think that sexual intercourse with animals is a misuse of the human body since such acts cannot result in issue.

Bestiality does not seem to harm animals but it can prevent some human beings from being able to have satisfactory sexual relations with other people. This danger is also present in people who are dependent on fetishes for their sexual pleasure.

Fetishes

Fetishes can be fun and are quite harmless so long as they help people towards establishing loving relationships. They become destructive when they get between two people who are trying to love each other so that one partner comes to feel that she or he is not there as a person for the other partner, who is obsessed by the fetish.

Transvestism is probably most commonly a form of fetishism, although other factors may contribute to its development. It affects more men than women and is particularly common among men who have had a close relationship with their mothers and have learnt to associate the soft feel of her clothing with emergent sexual feelings. Some of these men enjoy cross-dressing as a way of becoming sexually aroused but they are then able to enjoy full sexual intercourse with a woman. They are fortunate if they can find sexual partners who are not upset by their particular way of getting roused. Other men and their partners are very distressed by their behaviour and seek help. Behavioural techniques can help some of these people, but the condition is well known to be difficult to cure. It has no relationship with transexualism or homosexuality *per se*.

Fetishes are often tangible objects, like leather, fur, rubber articles of clothing. Some people, however, channel a great deal of their sexual energy into their work, their hobbies and their religious practices. Some of these people become so obsessed by their chosen love-objects that they have little energy left over to give to other human beings. They can be said to have made fetishes of their work, hobbies or religious rituals, even though they may not experience any overt sexual feeling when they are working, enjoying their hobbies or carrying out their religious duties.

The plight of people who can relate sexually only to animals and objects is obvious. Many of them are condemned to loneliness and a real impoverishment if they cannot share any real experience of love with other human beings. Their preoccupation with non-human objects sometimes makes them despise other people. Their increasing isolation can even make them devalue themselves as people. They may come to regard their own form of sexual behaviour as preferable to love. This attitude, which divorces sexual experience from love, is also shared by many of those who make extensive use of pornographic material in their lives.

Pornography

Many more men than women use pornographic material as a stimulus to promote sexual arousal, excitement and orgasm. One reason for this must be the fact that men respond more easily than women to visual sexual stimuli, and much pornography is visual in type. Another reason may be that men are still conditioned to be dominant in behaviour. They are usually expected to take the initiative in making sexual advances to women. Isolated, shy or timid men may find it very difficult to approach women, especially when the women appear to invite intimacy. Such men may turn instead to various sensate images as a substitute source of pleasure which can be enjoyed without the necessity of coming into contact with the dreaded objects of their affections.

Some people think that photographs or descriptions of nude or half-clothed human beings are pornographic in themselves, but they are a tiny minority. Most people agree that material can be described as pornographic only if it displays the genitalia and acts of sexual intercourse in ways that are calculated to excite a person sexually and prompt him or her towards orgasm. Pornographic material which is 'soft' exploits people's bodies for monetary gain. The term covers all material which does not explicitly link sexual behaviour with acts of violence.

There is no definite evidence to show that healthy people are corrupted by 'soft' pornography. It does, however, tend to keep immature or sick people in bondage to their fantasies which are the stock-in-trade of 'porn' magazines, 'blue movies', strip-tease shows and some night-club entertainments.

Sexually titillating 'soft' pornography of this kind can undoubtedly help some men and women to cope with their sexual needs with the minimum damage to themselves and other people, although any society which has to rely on pornography as a substitute for effective personal help must feel itself to be inadequate.

It is the association of sexual impulses with aggressive drives in 'hard' pornography that is responsible for people's greatest anxieties about all pornography, although nowadays the exploitation of children in the production of pornographic material is also causing a good deal of worry. This latter issue will be dealt with later in this chapter in the section on pederasty.

Pornographic material which is 'hard' deliberately focuses on people's sado-masochistic urges. It exploits these impulses by depicting sexual behaviour and intercourse in association with images or acts of violence like whips, bondage and rape.

Sado-masochism

The association between violence and sexual arousal is well known and is always openly exploited by those who market 'hard' porn. It is, however, increasingly apparent that violence is being used subliminally in all kinds of art, books, films and plays, which are not categorized as pornographic, in order to stimulate the audience sexually. Westerners are now so familiar with real and fantasy violence that relatively benign violence has ceased to act as a sexual stimulus to most people. The result is that more powerful stimuli in the form of more extreme portrayals of sado-masochistic situations are used by some entertainers in their attempts to stimulate their audiences' jaded appetites. Most people absorb these sado-masochistic stimuli without too much difficulty, but some women and men become so sexually excited by them that they feel a compulsion to act out their fantasies.

These compulsive fantasies can be very frightening. People are afraid of what they might do if they lost their self-control, and it is this fear that frequently drives people to seek help.

Those who come to friends or professional counsellors about their sexual fantasies often find it difficult to discuss their problems. They need to test their chosen counsellors before they confide in them. They can do this in several different ways. Some people, for instance, approach the topic of their sado-masochistic fantasies by asking their confidants for their opinions on some allied topic or event which is reported in the media. They often wait to talk about their real problems until their time for discussion has nearly run out. On the other hand, some people with sado-masochistic problems are so anxious about them that they launch themselves into a detailed description of their problem at the earliest opportunity. These people use precipitate confessions as a way of being able to discover whether or not their confidants are shock-proof and unprejudiced.

The time spent in helping reticent people to talk about themselves or in listening to precipitate confessions is well spent, for it is essential for counsellors to establish good rapport with clients who have sado-masochistic problems. Once such rapport has been established it is necessary for clients and counsellors to decide what they consider to be normal and what abnormal in this area of human experience where pain and pleasure mingle.

Pleasurable pain in moderation is acceptable to most people in their daily lives. Food, for instance, tastes better when people are hungry than when they are sated. Sexual appetites are whetted by abstinence and to some extent by resistance. A tantalizing modicum of pain during sexual intercourse gives pleasure to many women and men. They may, for instance, enjoy biting their sexual partners. They may get pleasure out of slapping and fighting, chasing and being chased, dominating and being dominated. People who have mild sadistic or masochistic tendencies sometimes find that a little cruelty acts as an aphrodisiac. They may enjoy sexual intercourse more if they can find a partner who complements their need, so that, for instance, one of them can enjoy beating the other who likes being beaten, or both can feel pleasure if they indulge each other's needs in bondage rituals. Most people would accept this kind of behaviour as normal. Abnormal sadists, however, seldom want masochistically inclined partners. Their pleasure is heightened when they inflict their cruelties on unwilling victims. Similarly, abnormal masochists do not seek out sadistically inclined partners. Instead they pick on kindly people who have no intention of hurting anyone. Sick masochists can make the most gentle person feel guilty of refined cruelty. Their victims may do their utmost to prove their love for the masochists, but the more they try the less they succeed and the greater the pleasure for the masochist.

Sadists and masochists may live in fantasy worlds or they may act out their fantasies in real life. The distinction is important, and one of the tasks facing those who help people with their problems is to establish how much sado-masochistic energy can be used up in the fantasy world or translated into normal sexual activity and how much is feeding anti-social and perverted behaviour. Very detailed histories of sado-masochistic people need to be taken if counsellors are to do justice to their clients.

When they are put at ease by experienced counsellors clients find great relief in confessing facts about themselves of which they are afraid and ashamed. Counsellors can often reassure their clients about the universality and comparative normality of most sado-masochistic fantasies and masturbatory or other sexual ruminations. They can also help the majority of their clients to realize that many compulsive feelings can be defused by self-stimulation or relational sexual activity which can channel their client's sexual energy in safe directions. When a compulsion cannot be fed by fear it often loses its grip on a person's psyche.

Counsellors have to recognize, however, that there are some compulsions which are so strong that they are capable of breaking the strongest will. Sooner or later those who are afflicted by very strong and compulsive sado-masochistic fantasies which are not ameliorated by masturbation or sexual intercourse are likely to indulge in destructive and anti-social behaviour. The danger of this happening is greatly increased when people operate in groups rather than as individuals. Cruelty is infectious and people will do things together which they might never consider if left to themselves. Rough sexual play, 'gang-bangs' and even forcible intercourse and rape seem to be more acceptable to a person when other people are involved in the humiliation and degradation of their victims. The individual conscience finds it difficult to stand out against the powerful feelings generated by a group of like-minded people.

Sexual drives used in this destructive way are unpleasant and dangerous when let loose on unsuspecting victims, yet many indecent assaults and rapes could be prevented if the warning signs of stong fantasy, compelling ruminations and a tendency to seek peer-group acceptance at any cost were to be recognized early enough so that preventive treatment could be offered to those who need help.

People with severe sado-masochistic impulses need formal psychiatric help, which may include drug therapy, rather than counselling, and their treatment falls outside the scope of this book, but it is vital that counsellors do not hold on too long to clients who are not coping with powerful compulsive sado-masochistic urges when there are signs that they are being acted out in real life situations.

Sexual violence

It is known that in some people and families violence and sexual intercourse are closely associated.

Only a few men end up in courts because they have raped or indecently assaulted other men, women or children, either on their own, or with a group of like-minded men. A far larger number of men are known to coerce unwilling sexual partners to submit to intercourse through the threat of violence. In an important book on the topic of rape, an American journalist, Susan Brownmiller, closed her opening chapter by stating:

Man's discovery that his genitalia could serve as a weapon to generate fear must rank as one of the most important discoveries of prehistoric times, along with the use of fire and the first crude stone axe. From prehistoric times to the present, I believe, rape has played a critical function. It is nothing more or less than a conscious process of intimidation by which *all* men keep *all* women in a state of fear.[3]

This is a strong statement, and its universalist application can be challenged, but certainly slightly built men, most women and nearly all children feel afraid when confronted by a sexually roused, aggressive man whose only interest is in his own sexual pleasure whether or not his intended partner is willing to receive his sexual advances.

The threat of violence alone can induce many people to submit to sexual intercourse in the hope of reducing the violent urges of a sexually roused individual. The potential victim knows that badly timed or ill-advised resistance can result in physical violence in which the weaker person is likely to be battered, maimed or even killed by a frustrated and enraged person.

Although a proportion of those involved in sexual violence are sadists or masochists, cruelty may not be a direct cause of the physical assault at all. Nor is the problem solely one in which women and children are always the victims of men. People of all kinds of ages, including some children, are capable of responding to the frustration of their sexual drives with a display of verbal and physical violence which may do considerable damage to those against whom it is directed.

Violent behaviour which is associated with sexual tensions of various kinds is a sign which always needs to be taken seriously. A good deal of domestic violence is of this kind, for instance, although there are often other factors which also contribute to the eruption of violence within the home. The work of well-established organizations such as the N.S.P.C.C., and of pioneers like Erin Pizzy,[4] on domestic violence needs to be consulted for more details, but it is well known that those adults who were battered as children, or who witnessed violence between their parents, are predisposed towards becoming the kind of people who batter or are battered. It is also known that poor social conditions, such as inadequate housing, overcrowding, penury and unemployment contribute to the genesis of domestic violence. People who are mentally disturbed or who are suffering from emotional illnesses, recent upheavals or disasters in their personal lives are also at risk. Sexual tensions may precipitate violence, but they are rarely the sole cause of the trouble, and counsellors will always need to explore all the circumstances which may have led to the deterioration in the personal relationships of people living together and behaving violently to each other because of sexual frustration.

Overt violence between sexual partners or between parents and children, can yield to treatment, which must always include attention to each individual's needs, environment and circumstances. In some respects overt violence may be less damaging to people than some of the fears which can develop in them in response to the threat of violence.

95

The threat of violence underlies many sexual relationships, and a great many people fall victim to it at some time during their lives. Many adults, for instance, can still remember occasions during their childhood when they were both thrilled and frightened by the sight of the exposed genitals of an adult male, the touch of a too-familiar relative, the sight or feel of an erect penis. Many children know the secret terror of being the object of another child's sexual desire. Some have found it difficult to extract themselves from a youthful homosexual relationship. Many adults are alarmed by incestuous feelings within their own family although relatively few people will have experienced an overt sexual relationship with a parent, sibling or close relative. The threat of violence can also affect marriages. A substantial number of women are afraid of their husbands and agree to have sexual intercourse when they have no desire for it themselves because they feel that something dreadful will happen if they refuse.

These reactions of fear to the violent potential of human sexuality can be very destructive to the development of mutual trust and love between sexual partners. Moreover, fear on either side of a sexual relationship can hinder the personal growth of each partner, or even stop it altogether.

The victims of sexual violence, whether it is overt or covert, often find that their experience of violence in one set of circumstances has a permanent spill-over effect on the rest of their lives. Women who have been raped, for instance, sometimes continue to feel polluted. Their fear of one man can become a general fear of all men. Their revulsion against intercourse on one occasion may prevent them from ever forming a happy sexual relationship with anyone else. Similarly, married women who have been coerced into sexual intercourse for any reason tend to respond to emotional blackmail in other areas of their life in the same way. They may become emotionally stunted and unable to relate maturely to other human beings even when they have escaped from their original blackmailer. Children who have been sexually assaulted or been the victims of incest, tend to grow up into adults who feel guilty about enjoying sexual intercourse.

It is not only the victims of sexual violence who are injured; those who commit violence against others suffer as well. After an eruption of sexual aggression they are often astonished at their actions, ashamed of their behaviour and alarmed lest it should happen again. Fear of their own strength, their capacity for violence, their selfishness, can lead to their withdrawal from social activity, to isolation or to despair which may manifest itself in profound depression or even suicide. A few people react to their own feelings of unhappiness by pretending that they do not care at all about their destructive behaviour. They boast about it or they show no concern for their victims. This indifference towards another person's suffering may extend itself into becoming a general hardening of attitude against allowing any emotion of gentleness, compassion or love to interfere with their own need for sexual gratification.

There is no easy cure for those who are given to sexual violence, nor for those who are its victims. The fact of violence has to be recognized, faced and lived through. There are some wounds that do not heal properly. In any case the scars are a perpetual reminder of past pain, present suffering and future limitations. Those who are scarred may continue to grow in spite of their memories, but a few people cannot allow their wounds to heal at all. They continue to pick at them and seem determined to suffer. In the end those who counsel such people have to decide whether or not they are fulfilling a therapeutic function by allowing their clients to indulge their self-pity and to perpetuate their revenge by refusing to enjoy present or future relationships.

People's punitive attitudes towards themselves and sexual intercourse in general may arise from their experience of sexual violence, but this is by no means always so. Counsellors frequently encounter people who punish others or themselves for no apparent reason, and although such behaviour has links with violence it needs dealing with in its own right.

Punitive sexual habits

When people feel guilty about real or imagined sins or have been hurt by unhappy sexual experiences they sometimes get into the habit of punishing themselves or other people. Guilt-ridden people who are conscious of past mistakes or sins may, for instance, try to deprive themselves of further pleasure by abstaining from sexual intercourse. Some of these people may try to resume sexual relations but their conscious or sub-conscious guilty feelings may prevent them from being able to enjoy their sexual activity properly. Counsellors will often meet clients who are able to have sexual intercourse but are unable to reach orgasm because of emotional blocks which induce them to punish themselves, and, incidentally, their partners.

There are another group of people who do not feel particularly guilty but who dislike their sexuality so much that they regard intercourse itself as a punishment. They despise their need for orgasm, deprive themselves of it for as long as possible and only concede to it when nature bursts out of its mentally imposed chains. Some individuals in this group carry this attitude towards sexuality to its extremes by turning dislike into virtue. They seem to delight in their ability to abstain from sexual activity because it signifies that they are superior to the common herd or more spiritually minded than their partners whose sexual advances have to be tolerated rather than welcomed.

The habit of regarding sexual intercourse as an unpleasant experience is sometimes responsible for the non-consummation of a marriage or other sexual relationship. This unhappy consequence of a potentially loving

98

relationship is a cruel punishment for both partners. It is surprising to learn how much suffering can be tolerated within such an unconsummated relationship before one or both partners seek outside help. Even when such help is sought the magnitude of the problem is not always appreciated. It is still common to hear of men and women being given the advice to 'get a little tipsy, and it'll be all right on the night', or told to, 'watch a few blue movies', or to 'take these pills and they'll help you along'.

It is not always easy to understand the intense psychological barriers which sometimes operate in people who continue to insist that they want to remain in a loving relationship with their chosen partners although they cannot tolerate the physical contact. Some of these clients succeed in persuading their partners to remain with them for long periods of sexual torment. Where the inability to consummate a sexual relationship is due to mistaken or self-punitive attitudes towards sexual intercourse the condition can be resolved by careful education and retraining programmes, but the treatment of a non-consummated sexual relationship is less likely to be successful when the condition is a long-established habit, is used as a way of punishing the partner over a long period of time, or when the motivation to get better is not high.

Less extreme forms of such punitive attitudes towards sexual intercourse can be found among sexual partners who have once enjoyed each other's sexuality, but who, for a variety of reasons, come to use this part of their relationship in a punitive way. One partner can cause the other dreadful misery through withholding sexual intercourse, or finding all kinds of excuses to postpone it. Sometimes the punitive partners know what they are doing and delight in behaving in that way. More often, however, they are aware of the pain they are causing and do not approve of their own attitudes.

A large number of men and women consult their doctors, counsellors and friends each year because they find that they no longer enjoy sexual intercourse and are rejecting their companions. They are well aware that they are in danger of destroying their partnerships through their inability to welcome sexual contact with those whom they once adored. Punitive attitudes are not, of course, always responsible for this kind of rejecting behaviour. Refusal to have sexual intercourse, impotence or frigidity may be due to other physical or psychological diseases, endocrine inbalance, tiredness, preoccupation with other interests or poor social conditions, and these factors have to be eliminated or taken into account whenever counsellors are trying to help clients who seem to be acting in punitive ways.

People who punish others often grow insensitive to the pain they inflict. People who need to be punished often insist on provoking punishment. So counsellors who try to help clients who are using their sexuality punitively have a difficult task. They may have to wait for a considerable time before they get a suitable opportunity to interpret their clients' destructive behaviour to them in a loving and unthreatening way. Once clients have gained insight into their punitive habits they can learn to give up their punitive behaviour in favour of the greater pleasure of enjoying happiness—either their own or other people's.

Promiscuity

People who live in western countries are so familiar with the concept of the importance of personal freedom that they tend to develop liberal attitudes towards casual and promiscuous sexual relationships.

Men and women sometimes form casual sexual relationships simply because they are hungry for experience. Alternatively, they may be curious about other people; they use sexual intercourse as a way of getting to know more about acquaintances who interest them. Some people are too isolated or too frightened to enter into long-term relationships with others, and they may think that 'one night stands' may help them to discover who they are and how they appear to outsiders.

Many modern men and women no longer feel it to be immoral to have sexual intercourse with many people during the course of their lives. Counsellors will also meet a number of people who do not feel guilty at all about their sexual involvements with other human beings. They are quite prepared to form casual and promiscuous relationships even though their lovers may already have responsibilities and binding relationships with other sexual partners, and even though they know that their new liaisons may destroy previously happy relationships. Many promiscuous people assert that established partnerships should not be threatened by casual, extra-marital (or extra-contractual) sexual intercourse, or promiscuous sexual relationships, and that it is the jealous partner's own fault if the partnership is disrupted by such passing adventures.

There are now signs, however, which suggest that the liberal attitudes which have been current in western society over the past two decades are being replaced by sterner attitudes towards promiscuity.

Judging from the available evidence, which includes that of a continuing decline in church attendance, the revulsion against liberalism is not a result of a return to the observance of religious practices so much as of a realistic appraisal of the consequences of promiscuity. These include an increase in venereal disease of all kinds, which may leave permanent effects such as irreversible sterility. Women who are promiscuous do not always realize their danger, since a disease like gonorrhoea can sometimes damage the reproductive system without declaring itself openly by obvious symptoms. The replacement of penile sheaths and cervical caps by oral contraceptives and intra-uterine devices has meant that veneral disease is more easily transmitted than used to be the case before the advent of the 'pill' and the 'coil'. Men are usually more aware of the symptoms of venereal diseases than are women, but in them, too, the late consequences of such diseases like urethral stricture, chronic epididymo-orchitis and generalized syphilis may not declare themselves for many years after the original infection.

Doctors are confronted too often by women who have enjoyed their sexual freedom until they want children, and have then found themselves unable to conceive because their fallopian tubes are blocked. This is a tragedy which is avoidable in many cases, but until now most health educators have failed to impress young people with the dangers of frequent sexual intercourse with different partners.

Promiscuity is not necessarily linked with irresponsible attitudes towards reproduction, but some promiscuous people are also feckless about contraception. Consequently, some women may become pregnant more often than they wish. Irresponsible men do not find it too difficult to be lighthearted about unwanted pregnancies, but women cannot escape so easily for they must resort to abortion if they do not feel able to bear children every time they get pregnant. Abortion is a destructive episode in people's lives. It is not, of course, confined to those who are promiscuous so it will be discussed separately, but in the context of promiscuity it should be noted that repeated abortion, whether natural or induced, can result in the inability of the uterus to retain pregnancies when eventually these women wish to become mothers.

Inflammatory pelvic disease is only one of the genito-urinary disease hazards which face promiscuous women and men. Venereal warts, scabies and body lice are common among people who exchange their sexual partners frequently. Syphilis may lie dormant for many years before it surfaces unpleasantly in crippling and death-dealing attacks on the blood vessels, heart, brain and spinal cord. There has been a statistical increase in cancer of the cervix among women who have started having sexual intercourse in their early and mid-teens, and this is more marked among those who have been pregnant, especially in those women who have had a high number of abortions or live births.

The emotional effects of promiscuity are not so well documented as the physical ones, and it is difficult to assess whether promiscuous women and men behave as they do because they have never been able to form stable loving relationships with one or two sexual partners, or whether they become incapable of lasting and satisfactory relationships because of their habitual promiscuity. Moreover, it is not at all easy to determine how much effect social attitudes and pressures have on people's sexual behaviour. It is known, for instance, that homosexual men exchange sexual partners more often than lesbians, but it is not known whether this is because of an innate difference between men's and women's attitudes towards sexual intercourse and its relationship to love and affection, or because of society's double standards towards female and male promiscuity, which affects all men and women whether they be 'straight' or 'gay'. Women's lives have been revolutionized by the discovery of effective contraceptives and the development of safer methods of sterilization, and it may be that they are as innately capable of promiscuity as men have always been acknowledged to be. In time society will probably learn to accept only one standard of behaviour in both sexes instead of condoning promiscuity in men and punishing it or condemning it in women, as happens at present in all western societies which legislate about prostitution.

Prostitution

Prostitution highlights the way in which society makes provision for promiscuity. It is possible to be very promiscuous without resorting to prostitution, but prostitutes could not survive economically unless there was a flourishing market for their saleable goods.

Western society on the whole tolerates prostitution although some countries seek to restrict it by punishing those who sell their sexual favours, namely the prostitutes and pimps. In countries which seek to control prostitution rather than to restrict or diminish it, licences are issued to prostitutes, who are subject to periodic health checks, rather than to those who pay for sexual intercourse. Countries which do not attempt either to limit or licence prostitution do not usually bother to protect either those who sell or those who buy at the market place. The onus of responsibility is placed firmly upon the buyer and the purveyor of sexual intercourse.

Anyone who listens to other people's life stories will sometimes feel deeply concerned about the way in which human beings are exploited sexually for commercial gain. Men and women are often manipulated into buying what they do not really want because of the way in which the goods on sale are displayed. Prostitutes of both sexes are mercilessly exploited and misused by those with whom they consort. It is easy to think of prostitution as an activity which degrades those who sell and those who buy sexual favours, yet counsellors who meet prostitutes and their customers will know that they are human beings with needs, sorrows and joys like everyone else. Many prostitutes and their customers have sexual problems which complement each other's sexual needs. A relationship which may appear to be very degrading to those outside it may be a source of mutual healing to the people who are relating to each other on a financial basis.

Most sexual counsellors are aware of the complex and ambivalent nature of prostitution. They do not, therefore, feel capable of tackling the community aspects of prostitution, so they confine themselves to working with individuals who ask for help because they are unhappy about their involvement with the 'oldest profession in the world', either as sellers or buyers of sexual favours.

It is impossible to tease out all the factors which impel individuals towards prostitution, but one important feature which is often found in both sellers and buyers is their poor opinion of their own worth despite the fact that both sets of people appear to boast about their sexual attractiveness and potency in different ways. This low self-esteem often makes people feel as if they are so degraded in the eyes of other people in society that they 'might as well be hanged for a sheep as for a lamb' and so they become an obvious target for any unscrupulous profiteers who want to make a lot of money and who do not mind what happens to those whom they exploit.

Prostitutes and/or their clients who want to develop more satisfying relationships than those based upon payment for services rendered can often be helped to achieve their objective if they can raise their opinion of themselves. In order to do this they may have to spend long periods of time with understanding and accepting counsellors as they painfully work through their feelings of self-disgust and self-condemnation and begin to find positive qualities within themselves on which they can build a new future. Their search for their own true identity, of which they can be rightly proud, may well involve them in a complete change of life-style, environment and work.[6]

Those who know a great deal about prostitution often say that it is all too easy for young men and women to go back on 'the game' when they find themselves in stressful situations of any kind. Turning away from a life of prostitution, or a compulsion to make use of a prostitute, is no more easy than turning away from cigarettes, drugs, alcohol and gambling is to addicts or compulsive gamblers. Counsellors must expect their clients to relapse into former patterns of behaviour from time to time, yet they will also know the value of frequent contact, constant encouragement and praise which can reinforce their client's emergent self-appreciation. It is also known that clients who join in self-help groups and small supportive discussion groups have the best chance of altering their behaviour.

Many people who know little about bestiality, fetishism, pornography, sado-masochism, sexual violence, punitive sexual behaviour, promiscuity and prostitution, apart from being aware of their potential destructiveness in people's lives, tolerate deviant sexual behaviour in society because they recognize that sexual behaviour is very variable, and they would like to give other people the same measure of freedom as they would like to think they have themselves.

At the same time many tolerant people feel mildly repelled by aberrant sexual behaviour when they read or hear about it, or when they meet someone whom they know to be sexually eccentric. According to temperament people may suppress their feelings of revulsion and become over-permissive in their attitudes towards variant sexual behaviour, or they may enhance their pleasurable disgust by voyeurish and scandalous gossip about other people's sexual adventures. However, once people can openly admit to their dislike of sexual behaviour when it becomes destructive to the dignity and happiness of human beings they can deal with their feelings in a constructive way.

Counsellors, like everyone else, are not immune from their emotional reactions to deviant sexual behaviour. They have to learn to accept the reality of such feelings, to allow for their presence and to control them so that they can be used objectively and properly in the service of their clients and the community.

In common with others, however, counsellors are likely to feel explosive when they encounter people who have violated certain strict rules of sexual behaviour which are widely accepted to be essential to the welfare of the whole human community. Most people condemn incest, for instance: almost all abhor the sexual violation of children.

Incest

The incest taboo exists to protect the human race from some inheritable diseases which might be transmitted to future generations through inbreeding. Having children by close relatives increases the risk of recessive genes becoming dominant and thus causing potential disease to become actual.

The incest taboo operates at a psychological level within families to enable the children to detach themselves from their parents, brothers and sisters in order to seek their mates from outside their immediate family circle. The taboo is broken when a parent has sexual intercourse with one of the children, or when the siblings mate with each other.

Although the moral prohibition of incest is strongly reinforced by stern social legislation, particularly in regard to fathers and daughters, it does not operate well when families are living in confined spaces and poor social circumstances, or when relations between the parents are unhappy. In any unstable society physical sexual intercourse between members of the same family is not uncommon, and counsellors will encounter incestuous relationships quite frequently in the course of their work.

Apart from its adverse genetic consequences incest can damage emotional health. Many of those who are sexually immature when they are involved in incestuous relationships later find it very difficult or even impossible to form satisfactory sexual relationships with other people. Young adults who have had sexual intercourse with members of their own family often suffer from feelings of anxiety, guilt, depression and self-recrimination. Older adults often live in fear of discovery. They are vulnerable to blackmail.

Incest is often concealed. Exposure can lead to the prosecution of the offending adults. Many doctors, psychologists, health visitors and social workers keep quiet about their knowledge of incestuous relationships. They do so because they know that the emotional upheaval which follows discovery can sometimes do more damage than the liaison itself. Members of the caring professions naturally shrink from being party to the kind of sudden rupture in relationships that happens, for instance when a father finds himself in prison for making his thirteen-year-old daughter pregnant, and she finds herself in care in a mother-and-baby home without being fully able to understand why the love between her and her father was so wrong. So, sometimes counsellors who learn about incestuous relationships in the course of their work keep that knowledge to themselves while they try to help the people involved to effect a gradual and more natural emotional separation from each other. There is always a risk in taking this course of action, for incest is a criminal offence, so to conceal it is to be an accessory to crime, but some counsellors feel that they should never reveal anything they have learned in the course of their work, so they act according to their conscience and accept the consequences if they are found out.

Although physical incest is widely condemned, psychological incest attracts less attention. This is partly due to the fact that many people in western society now take it for granted that sexuality is the driving force which underlies all deep emotional attachments between fathers and daughters, mothers and sons. Western attitudes towards the emotional development of children are still heavily influenced by the theories of Sigmund Freud. It is obviously important for counsellors to acquire a good working knowledge of the 'oedipal' and 'electra' theories and there is plenty of good material about the Freudian outlook on personality development which is available to students who wish to pursue the matter further.[7]

Freud's theories have gained fairly wide acceptance in western society and they are often cited in discussions about parent-child relationships, especially where childhood experiences are thought to affect adult emotional responses and behaviour. These theories need to be complemented by an equally good understanding of behaviourist and Gestalt theories about personality development.[8] Knowledge about all these theories could, for instance, be helpful to a counsellor who is trying to work out exactly why a particular young woman is unable to have a good sexual relationship with her husband and is constantly having rows with him about the amount of time she spends at her parent's home. Such a tug-of-war between a husband and a father for the affections of a woman is a real problem that may not yield easily to explanation however adequate the theory. Many counsellors find that they have to know all the theories, and then tuck them into the back of their minds in favour of a common-sense approach to the very prevalent problem of psychological incest.

It is an undeniable fact that most parents have a deep emotional investment in their children. Unless the sexual relations between the parents are satisfying, one or other of them, or both, will tend to channel more of their sexual energy into their love for their children than they would have done were it to be directed towards and fully accepted by their spouses. Children respond readily to this kind of hidden sexual love. They return it freely and innocently. They may discover the depth of their own feelings only when the time comes for them to give their whole-hearted love to someone right outside their own family. Their new relationship may suffer because of their painful feelings about breaking away emotionally from their parents. People who suffer from divided loyalties in this way may be so handicapped that they may become permanently emotionally crippled. Some of them never leave their parents. They never marry, nor do they establish their independence. Some of them leave home physically, but they remain emotionally tied to it and they never feel completely happy anywhere else. This kind of emotional imprisonment can be self-inflicted, or it can be unconsciously imposed on children by parents who mis-interpret their own possessiveness as natural concern for their children's happiness. Many potentially successful marriages have ended in divorce, for instance, simply because the emotional separation between parents and children, which usually takes place during adolescence, was never satisfactorily and lovingly accomplished.

Psychological incest is common and most counsellors will quickly acquire the ability to see when it is happening. They will probably be able to see the solutions to the problem long before their clients can. The time spent in getting to the point where separation from the parents can be achieved without disaster is well spent as people in this kind of situation often have the potential for rapid growth towards psychological integration once they have estab-lished their emotional independence. Their parents, too, will often find that the friendship of their mature children can be more precious than the helpless dependence that is characteristic of immature people who refuse to grow up.

It is always right to aim for a successful resolution of a problem which arises out of psychological incest, but unfortunately it has to be admitted that there are many people who remain crippled by emotional incest, whether they be parents, children or siblings.

Counsellors often feel distressed by their failure to solve such emotional problems because their own feelings are disturbed by their client's apparent inability to take the necessary decisions that would resolve their unhappiness. Experienced counsellors can always recall horror stories about people whom they have been unable to help in these kinds of destructive situations. Most counsellors can, how-ever, learn to accept their inevitable failures without too much guilt or anxiety. They find it much more difficult to cope with their own feelings when they meet a pederast or child molester.

Pederasty

Adults are well aware of the beauty of innocence. Many grown-up people find children beautiful because of their innocence, and some discover themselves to be sexually roused by young boys and girls. There is nothing particularly startling about this, but all the same many people are dismayed when they find themselves so susceptible to youthful bodies, and the younger the children are the more upsetting this can be.

Most people in society cope with their sexual feelings towards their own and other people's young children by using strong taboo feelings to help them to direct their sexual energies in more appropriate ways. Indeed, this kind of displacement is so common that many adults are unaware of their sexual interest in children until they hear of someone else's assault on a young child. Some people will then find themselves overwhelmed by angry and punitive feelings towards the child molester. They feel they would willingly kill or mutilate the offender because they feel obliged to condemn in other people feelings of which they would be afraid if they recognized them in themselves.

Such extreme reactions to child molesters are uncommon, perhaps, but to a lesser degree nearly everyone in society feels distressed when they read or hear about indecent exposure, sexual assault, rape and sexually motivated murder where the victims are children. Most people in society feel that there are good reasons for discouraging adults from having sexual intercourse with children. One good reason is that pre-pubertal children are not equipped to cope with the powerful feelings of adolescents and mature adults. Children's emotional lives may be permanently injured if they have to relate sexually to other people before they are developed enough to know what is happening to their own bodies and feelings. It is known, for instance, that boys who have been sexually assaulted when very young, or even at school by older boys or trusted adults, can become very twisted individuals when they mature. As adults, some of them find themselves unable to relate to sexual partners unless there is a sado-masochistic component to the relationship. Girls can be affected in much the same way, but they suffer more than men from their guilt complexes. This is because society in general still tends to blame girls and women more than men whenever unlawful sexual intercourse takes place. They are often accused of inviting men to molest them. These accusations are sometimes difficult to refute. They may be internalized. Consequently many girls and women who have been innocent victims of savage sexual assault still blame themselves for their misfortune. Their false sense of guilt sometimes destroys their ability to enjoy sexual intercourse with anyone.

Pederasty is condemned by most people in western society. The current hostility towards pederasts and self-confessed paedophiles has driven many of them into hiding and they have to cope with their sexual urges as well as they can. Some of them undoubtedly resort to pornography for relief.

The exploitation of children for the production of pornographic magazines and films is indefensible, although it is often said that such material helps paedophiles to fantasize during masturbation and so prevents them from assaulting little children. If that is so, then ample material already exists which could satisfy their needs and no more children need to be degraded in order to produce new material. It is precisely because children do not understand the implications of what they are being asked to do, or how they are being asked to pose, that they are in need of protection. Exploiters will always say that the children enjoy themselves and so they may at the time, but children have memories. It is the association of sub-conscious and half-recalled infantile memories with adult feelings and experiences which can produce overwhelming shame in later years, or alternatively a defiant shame-lessness which springs from the same origins.

Paedophiles and pederasts certainly need all the help they can get but that help cannot be at the expense of children who cannot give their consent to the use of their bodies for other people's sexual gratification. It is not easy to help those who are sexually attracted only by children's bodies and many counsellors feel inadequate for such a task. It is comforting, therefore, to realize that it is possible to learn by experience, that all competent counsellors were once incompetent, and that the majority of counsellors usually feel inadequate anyway.

Society expects more and more from its professional counsellors and anyone who has lived during this century must be astonished and pleased by the way in which the various services have expanded and developed to meet the increased challenges and demands made on them. Nowhere is this growth more apparent than in the fields of birth control, abortion and sterilization counselling, which are closely related to sexual counselling. Sexual counsellors may not wish to become involved with all the various technical aspects of fertility control, but they will inevitably find that anxieties about reproduction affect the sexual lives of many of their clients, so they will be drawn into the ethical aspects of the subject by their client's needs.

Destructive aspects of fertility control

Birth control

Some people believe that any form of birth control is destructive. They hold that it is wrong to have sexual intercourse and yet try to prevent conception from occurring, since, to their way of thinking, God's purposes for the human race in general, and for the individuals concerned in particular, might be thwarted by such an action. Most people who adopt this view, however, will tolerate sexual abstinence, either total or partial, as a legitimate way of fertility control. They make this exception because they accept the right of all people to listen to their own consciences as they try to fulfil God's will in their lives. At the same time they will accept the legitimacy of the appeal to conscience only if it is educated and informed, preferably by those who hold similar views to their own.

When people are willing to indoctrinate their children with such purist views, the children are likely to feel very guilty indeed if they subsequently go against their parents' wishes. Many Roman Catholics and others who have been brought up to think that 'artifical' birth control is morally wrong find themselves obliged to live with chronic guilt when they decide to limit their family, even when they are intellectually convinced of the rightness of birth control. Hence counsellors will meet clients who cannot fully enjoy sexual intercourse nor reach orgasm if they are using contraceptives. A substantial number of people will admit that they enjoy sexual intercourse more if they know that a pregnancy is possible than if they are using a very effective form of contraception like the 'pill'.

Counsellors will still meet a number of clients who have no moral inhibitions about using contraceptives but who nevertheless find that sexual intercourse is spoilt for them by contraceptive devices like sheaths, cervical caps, C-films, pessaries, oral contraceptives and intra-uterine devices of various kinds. There may be good reasons for this unhappy state of affairs, if, for instance, there is some physical reason for the discomfort, like an ill-fitting penile sheath or cervical cap, or an oral contraceptive which depresses a woman's libido or causes her to bleed between periods. Usually these problems can be resolved by simple alterations in contraceptive technique, but the difficulties will persist in a number of people and then the counsellor will have to probe further.

One of the commonest reasons for unhappiness about contraception is the very real anxiety many people feel about the dangers of some forms of contraception. Counsellors will meet couples whose partnerships are ruined by their fear of the woman's becoming very ill or even dying because she is taking oral contraceptives, or has a hormone implant or is using an intra-uterine device. Counsellors can meet these kinds of fear with practical help only by giving their clients the information they need to enable them to make up their own minds as to which of the relative risks they wish to accept in regard to contraception.

Counsellors encounter one less agreeable aspect of their work when their clients get pregnant and then ask for the pregnancy to be terminated.

Abortion
Abortion is a destructive act with irreversible consequences for the foetus.

The ultimate objectives of the existing health services are that every pregnancy should be planned, every mother delivered of a healthy baby and every child born because it is wanted. That is why in a country like Britain contraception is free to the customer, mothers are encouraged to deliver their babies under the safest possible conditions, and maternity and child benefits are given to parents so that they are relatively free from financial anxiety at the time of the birth. Unfortunately such enlightened attempts to reach the ideal are undermined by the fact that many women and some families are too sick to bear children. In addition, some unborn children seem to be programmed for disaster for various reasons. Therapeutic abortion offers one solution to these kinds of problem.

Attitudes towards abortion vary from complete opposition to absolute insistence that every woman has the right to choose whether or not to bear a child. Society usually reflects majority attitudes through its legislation, and at present most western countries have legislation which allows for the therapeutic termination of pregnancies if the risk to the mother's life and/or health in continuing the pregnancy are greater than the risks of continuing the pregnancy.

Therapeutic abortion is also permitted if the foetus is known to be or is likely to be abnormal. Surgeons may operate to remove foetuses at any time before they are capable of separate existence from their mothers, but different countries set different time limits after which such procedures are forbidden by law. Many countries tighten their rules if the termination has to be carried out after the first ten to twelve weeks of pregnancy. Therapeutic abortion is also permitted in some countries, if the circumstances of a family are so adverse that there is a substantial risk that the existing children would be harmed by the advent of another child.[9]

Those countries which legislate for abortion have the satisfaction of seeing the maternal mortality rate fall because fewer women have to resort to 'back street' abortionists and so deaths are less frequent than formerly from haemorrhage, air embolism and sepsis. By now thousands of families and millions of women have had reason to be grateful for humane legislation. Nevertheless, therapeutic abortion does have some adverse short- and long-term consequences which matter, not only to the woman concerned, but also to society as a whole.

Despite adequate care some women still die from the complications of surgery. Some become sterile through sepsis. Others become prone to habitual abortion because of laxity at the neck of the womb. Counsellors will inevitably meet some women who have had one or two therapeutic abortions when young and who then find themselves unable to have children when they want to. Therapeutic abortions do not always have such disastrous consequences, of course, but at present it is very difficult to predict which women are likely to develop complications after such a relatively simple operation. It is known that disasters are multiplied when abortion is driven underground, and that repressive legislation does nothing to decrease post-abortion morbidity and sterility. The health of future generations of women depends upon the discovery of improved methods of birth control, better abortion techniques and surgical techniques for the correction of tubal diseases. It is unrealistic to envisage a time in the near future when abortion will become redundant.

The possible physical consequences of therapeutic abortion are well known. The psychological consequences are less well understood because of the difficulty of establishing the links between cause and effect. Observers often seem to lose their critical faculties when they enter this field of study. Some say that therapeutic abortion leaves no psychological scars at all if it is done for the right reasons, by the right people in the right way. Other people insist that a large number of women and some men suffer from prolonged guilt and depression because of their involvement in abortions. The most objective observers admit that some parents become ill, either soon after an abortion, or in later life. Their illnesses are related to the abortions, but it is difficult to say whether they are ill because of their actions, or ruminating guiltily about their actions because they are ill. Whatever the reason, these people are psychologically disturbed by a crisis event in their lives, and they need help rather than criticism.

Abortion and post-abortion counselling is a demanding occupation which deserves time and care. The potential mother is often subjected to outside pressures. The potential father is often forgotten or neglected. The immediate relatives often need help themselves if they are to cope with their own feelings of distress. The unborn children cannot speak for themselves and they are generally represented only by emotionally involved adults or prejudiced outside opinion. In the circumstances it is not surprising that counsellors sometimes adopt an all-or-nothing approach to the whole subject, either acceding to any request within the spirit of the law or refusing to have anything at all to do with abortion.

Doctors who believe that it is right for them to share the responsibility of making decisions about abortions with the parents concerned carry a heavy burden even if they decide to surrender the final choice to the pregnant woman. The woman herself carries an equally burdensome weight of responsibility, for it is she who has to ask for or consent to an abortion in the first place.

At present in a country like England, where the pressure from overseas visitors, who cannot get legal abortions in their own countries, is very heavy, there are far too many requests for abortions and far too few counsellors for the work to be done properly in all cases, but it is at least possible to administer the law humanely. For this to happen it is essential that counsellors should be able to take adequate note of their own prejudices and past experiences in their personal and professional lives. Some counsellors find this area of sexual counselling so disturbing that they wisely seek professional help in working through their own feelings about abortion.

Sterilization

Abortion is such a destructive act that by comparison sterilization seems almost creative. Sterilization is more effective than many forms of contraception and less hazardous than some, and because its failure rate is so low it virtually obviates the necessity for abortion. Nevertheless sterilization is a destructive act for it destroys a person's ability to reproduce. Hence it must be classified as a destructive aspect of sex, and because it is an act with final consequences it cannot be undertaken lightly.

Medical knowledge about the effects of sterilization on people is still in its infancy. Within the last twenty-five years social attitudes towards vasectomy and tubal ligation have changed a great deal. At the beginning of this period sterilization was considered only when there was a real threat to the life of a client. Women were not usually offered the operation until they were nearing the menopause. Vasectomy was almost unheard of. A few geneticists were willing to sterilize people who carried deadly genes which were likely to be transmitted to their offspring. But for the most part their enthusiasm was condemned. After all, their opponents argued, even such dreadful diseases as Huntingdon's chorea, which afflicts young people with premature senility, were known to affect only half the children and no one could tell which child was afflicted and which spared until the disease declared itself in adult life, nor was it possible to say who were carriers of the disease. The Roman Catholic Church was implacably opposed to sterilization, but the Anglican Church adopted a more low-key approach altogether and indicated that individual cases needed to be considered individually. The law was uncertain, but it was usual to secure the husband's consent before a woman could be sterilized.

The position is much changed today, partly because of the population explosion, partly because of the known hazards of contraception and partly because there has been a great change in social and moral attitudes towards the quality of life which women and children are expected to have as a birthright. At present all western countries provide medical services enabling people of either sex to be sterilized. Roman Catholic and Muslim leaders remain firmly opposed to sterilization but their adherents are now deciding these issues for themselves, and many feel it right for them to adopt this method of fertility control in their particular circumstances. Both partners are normally required to give their consent before one of them is sterilized, but the right of any individual to make that decision alone is increasingly claimed and recognized. Some of those who now ask for sterilization are very young at the time of their request. Some are unmarried people who have decided never to have children. The majority, however, are married people who have completed their families and who are not able to, or do not wish to, use less final forms of contraception. Provided that their clients understand the permanent nature of the operation and its possible complications, most doctors, other than those who think it wrong to interfere with anyone's reproductive function while they are still able to bear children, will accede to their request.[10] Doctors are, however, usually hesitant about sterilizing someone if they sense that the request is being made under excessive pressure from the other partner or a relative, if the marriage is patently unstable or if one of the couple concerned has a history of psycho-sexual disturbance. This is because it is well known that sterilization can precipitate a crisis in individuals or families when they are under strain.

Despite all the care which is taken before such operations are carried out things can and do go wrong. Some men who have had a vasectomy do not heed the request to have serial investigations of their semen after the operation to make sure that they have become sterile before they drop contraceptive precautions. (It may take three to four months before all the spermatozoa in the tubes distal to the cut *vas deferens* are dead or ejaculated.) So sometimes an unwanted pregnancy ensues. Other men who were very light hearted about the effects of operation before it took place develop painful scrotal bruising and feel so alarmed that they become temporarily impotent. Others suddenly and unexpectedly find that they are more affected by the knowledge that they are sterile than they expected. The volume of ejaculate produced after vasectomy is slightly smaller than before the operation and this worries some men. Others find themselves impotent for no apparent reason despite strong reassurance from surgeons and counsellors before and after the operation.

Women, too, suffer some consequences when they have been sterilized, even though they are left with virtually no external scars and no obvious evidence of their sterility. The risks from their having had operations remains higher than the dangers of vasectomy. Women occasionally die from the effects of the anaesthetic, or from internal haemorrhage or pulmonary emboli, and some of them develop serious pelvic infections. There is a very small failure rate to the operation (1 : 100,000) but that is no consolation to the unfortunate few who become pregnant after their operation.[11] Psychological sequelae are not infrequent and some women undoubtedly feel deprived of a part of their womanhood even though their menstrual periods appear normally and they continue to be able to enjoy orgasm.

These problems can usually be overcome with the aid of an attentive ear and a common-sense approach, but occasionally the sterilization has merely triggered off a previously hidden and more serious psychological or psychosexual disorder in one or both of the sexual partners. When it is seen that the problem does not really lie with the sterilization but is in the psyche, it is important for counsellors to wean their clients away from laying all the blame on to the operation as they often want to do. It is only when this side-tracking has been firmly stopped that proper attention can be given by counsellors and clients alike to the intra-psychic difficulties which are the real cause of the problem. From that point onwards it becomes possible to treat the difficulties in the same way as any other problem which is not linked to surgical intervention.

The convenience and relative simplicity of sterilization, has benefited many people but sterilization is also open to abuse. Some clients learn which answers will satisfy their doctors so they are sterilized, but later they come to regret their decision and ask for its reversal. Other clients are satisfied with their sterility but use it as an excuse for promiscuity. Some men and women become paranoid about their sterilization and accuse their spouses, medical advisers and counsellors of having pressurized them into taking a step which they feel they would not have taken on their own—or so they think, having completely forgotten what they were like at the time of the operation.

Clients are not the only people who abuse sterilization. Occasionally dreadful scandals hit the headlines. They reveal that doctors and close relatives have deliberately planned to sterilize children or dependants who cannot possibly understand the nature of the proposed operation. It is known that many well-intentioned but illegal operations have already been performed on mentally handicapped young people who were thought to be incapable of becoming effective parents. Parents and doctors have also been known to suggest hysterectomy as a way of sparing mentally or physically handicapped children the burden of menstruation.

There is also evidence to suggest that pressure amounting to blackmail is sometimes put on to women to be sterilized after therapeutic abortions. Some parents and doctors become very impatient with girls who repeatedly get pregnant and then ask for termination of their unwanted pregnancy. Older adults can feel very punitive towards these young women whom they often accuse of being promiscuous, irresponsible and careless. Sometimes these punitive attitudes are translated into threats which imply that the termination will not be carried out unless the women concerned agree to be sterilized at the same time. Desperate young women have been known to consent to any procedure in order to rid themselves of an unwanted foetus, but some of them suffer bitter regrets at a later stage of their lives. Some of these unfortunate women turn up at gynaecological clinics years later to ask if their operation can be reversed now that they have settled down and are happily married. A number of them have never told their husbands about their plight. Consequently they must live with their guilty secret and are terrified by the knowledge that discovery might lead to the break-up of their marriage.

It is obvious that people should never be pressurized

into making irreversible decisions when they are vulnerable because they are facing such a crisis in their lives. It is also well known that anyone's well-intentioned and kindly suggestions can be misunderstood by distraught people who think that they are confronted with a disaster, whether it be real or imaginary. Such misunderstandings can make them feel threatened when they are not being emotionally blackmailed at all. It is, therefore, usually wise for counsellors and doctors to refuse to sterilize anyone within the immediate context of an abortion or delivery of a child unless there has been an opportunity of discussing the issues at a less emotive time in their client's lives.

Sexual desire can be such a destructive force in people's lives that it is relatively easy for clients to become despondent about their problems and doubtful about their ability to find solutions to those problems.

Sexual counsellors can bring hope to their clients. They can help them to get their problems into perspective. They can encourage their clients to find ways of replacing the unhappiness of destructive sexual activity with the joy of creative sexual relationships. In order to help people with sexual problems, counsellors will need to know about and be able to enlist the help of various available kinds of sexual therapy.

FIVE
Sexual Therapy

From time to time clients who have formed good relationships with their counsellors will need more formal therapy as well as counselling. It is important for counsellors to know how to give such help or where it can be found if they are unwilling or unable to act as therapists themselves.

The difference between counselling and therapy

The distinction between counselling and therapy is not obvious to everyone, nor is it acceptable to all clients, counsellors and therapists. Nevertheless, a significant number do find the distinction useful, particularly since the role of the counsellor has changed and is still changing. There was a time, for instance, when counsellors were seen as people who gave directive advice based upon their knowledge and experience. That kind of parental role has been modified over the years so that now a counsellor is more often seen as a friend who 'engages in an enabling process designed to help an individual come to terms with his life as it is and ultimately to grow to greater maturity through learning to take responsibility and to make decisions for himself.'[1]

Many Christian counsellors, including the author, do not want to stop there. They believe that counselling can do more than help people to deal with their immediate problems. They know that it is important to be able to come to terms with reality and to grow to maturity by learning to make decisions, but their religious faith prompts them to believe that God is actively at work in their clients' lives. These Christian counsellors try to help their clients to see the Holy Spirit at work in every situation, even where there is much confusion, suffering and darkness. They try to work with the Spirit in encouraging people to want to grow towards a wholeness which lies beyond human expectation. They consider it to be important to help people to look at their problems within the wider context of human relationships and from the perspective of the ultimate purpose of their lives. And they are not afraid to encourage their clients to look for the finest qualities in themselves and, with God's help, to build the future on those foundations as they strive after their ideals.

The majority of present-day counsellors, whatever their faith, would certainly say that they do not aim to tell their clients what to do, but do aim at enabling them to become more mature and fulfilled people. It sometimes becomes quite obvious, however, that internal or external factors are preventing their clients from growing up and that treatment is needed before the enabling process can get under way again. A therapeutic or treatment relationship differs from a counselling one in that it is usually directed towards the removal of a specific disability which is preventing a person or family group from growing towards wholeness.

Ultimately counsellors and therapists share the same goals and the two roles overlap considerably, but the distinction remains helpful to many, though not to all, professional people working in both fields, for a deeper understanding of the limitations of each discipline can lead to a better use of skills and training in either or both kinds of relationship.

In general, then, counselling enables clients to clarify their problems. It helps people to look for the root causes of them and to take decisions which will enable them to be overcome or, on occasion, to accept the existence of problems in their lives without being defeated by them. It helps them to believe in the future. Counsellors tend to work with people able to function adequately in society, and they focus mainly on the conscious material presented to them by their clients, or on that which emerges because of the counselling relationship. They also observe and interpret inter-personal behaviour between themselves and their clients, and between the clients and other people in their social environment. Counsellors may also help their clients to remodel their behaviour by allowing this remodelling to develop with themselves and by encouraging the clients to try out their new-found skills in inter-personal relationships, initially within a safe environment, and later on in more hostile circumstances.

Therapists, by contrast, tend to work with people who can no longer function adequately in society, although sometimes the loss of function is confined to quite a narrow and specific area of the client's life. Therapists often use medical models to describe their work and they usually think of themselves as helping sick people. There are a wide range of aids, drugs and techniques to assist them in their task, and they are generally able to deal with unconscious material, disturbed behaviour and role problems at great length and in more detail than counsellors are. One distinguished family therapist sees his work in these terms:

The prime necessity is for the therapist to receive the projection without being taken over by it and acting it out, so that he can maintain his own identity and respond in a way which is related to the expectations inherent in the model projected, but which is different and, hopefully (if the therapist is more mature or healthy than the person on whom the original model was based) a more accurate and effective guide to dealing with the world. Sometimes the therapist is aware of such a projection as an alien force with which he has to struggle, while in other cases the struggle and choice may be less conscious and determined more by the discipline of good technique.[2]

Counsellors and therapists, whether they are paid for their work or do it without direct financial gain, are approached by clients who want help because they think that they have problems which warrant outside help. So at the outset of any problem-centred relationship, and usually before, that relationship has become well established, the counsellor and client have to decide whether the client is a well person with a tough problem or a sick person whose problem has proved to be the precipitating factor in the client's breakdown of health. Several interviews may be necessary before they are able to decide whether counselling or therapy is the more appropriate way of dealing with the situation.

There are really very few guide-lines to help people to decide whether or not they are ill. Sometimes it is quite obvious to counsellors that their clients have lost touch with reality. They may, for instance, hear voices which the counsellor cannot hear. They may suffer from delusional ideas which persuade them to believe that close relatives, friends or other people are persecuting them. They may be so depressed that they are unable to speak, or so anxious that they are unable to sit down for any length of time. In many instances a counsellor and client can agree with each other in deciding that one of them is ill. Sometimes, however, it is much harder to draw a line between normality and abnormality, and then the counsellor tends to fall back on his or her clinical judgement.

This clinical judgement about a client's relative health or sickness is determined to some extent by the counsellor's own upbringing, value-system and social conditioning. Since counsellors have a vested interest in believing themselves to be healthy and useful members of society they tend to accept the social norms currently acceptable to people like themselves who share their background, education and social status in society. Even if they rebel against their own interests and class, counsellors are often more heavily influenced by their cultural conditioning than they think. This means that some counsellors may label people's attitudes and behaviour as sick when others would think of these same people as healthy in relation to a sick society. The work of men like Laing, Illich and Szasz has shown many professional counsellors how difficult it is to know whether clients are ill or well in relation to a society which can be described as unhealthy or healthy according to the criteria adopted by those setting themselves up as the arbiters of community health norms.

Healing relationships

When clients come to experienced counsellors, either through the good offices of a friend or through professional referral, they do not usually know what to expect from the relationship. Many clients have quite unrealistic ideas about what can be achieved through counselling or therapy. Their ideas and expectations have an effect upon their counsellors which modifies the relationship from the outset. Counsellors and therapists are trained to be realistic about themselves, their clients and their treatments. Yet they are human beings themselves and they often respond to their clients' needs by becoming the kind of people who are able to attract shy and anxious people needing to be accepted rather than criticized in the initial stages of the therapeutic relationship. Consequently the effect of many complicated inter-relationships with clients is to alter the counsellors themselves, so that counsellors may adopt norms which are quite different from those prevalent in the society in which they and their clients have to live. Relatively unprejudiced, liberal-minded, educated counsellors often have real difficulty in realizing that their adopted norms are not as common as they would like to think. This means that some of their clients are not going to be able to find the kind of acceptance they enjoy within the therapeutic relationship when they leave the consulting room for the harsher realities of ordinary life.

Clients are fortunate indeed if they manage to find counsellors and therapists who are sympathetic to them yet sufficiently detached from them to be able to help them to cope with the everyday demands of life. The best kind of therapy, however, is not limited to helping clients to come to terms with their own limitations and their

128

different circumstances. It also involves freeing people from various chains which limit their potential so that they can develop their latent talents and grow into more fulfilled people.

Clients have a right to expect their counsellors to be realists and also practical people, the kind of people who are able and willing to help their clients to overcome various social disadvantages which they find oppressive. At one level the need for practical intervention is obvious. Most counsellors and clients would agree that it is useless to treat individuals without also tackling the environmental factors which contribute to their unhappiness. It is, for instance, very difficult to treat impotence and frigidity in an effective way when the couple concerned are living in overcrowded conditions where privacy is almost unknown. A well-written letter to the local housing authority is more likely to be helpful than, for instance, a detailed instruction in the special behavioural techniques devised by Masters and Johnston for the treatment of sexual inadequacy. Counsellors often give this kind of practical help to their clients and it is invaluable.

At another level of practical help, however, clients and counsellors are much less confident. Many of them tend to think that they can do relatively little about altering sick attitudes in society which oppress certain sections of the community. It is here that practical realism needs to be supplemented by the kind of confident determination and optimism that one might expect to be able to transform an oppressive society into a just one. Society has every reason to be grateful to all the people concerned: clients, counsellors and therapists, who have worked so hard to encourage individuals and communities to adopt more healthy attitudes towards people's sexual propensities and problems. Obviously, different individuals will have many different views about what constitutes a healthy attitude towards sexuality, but society can become what it is meant to be only if as many of its individual members as possible agree to be involved in shaping its moral attitudes, structures and laws.

On choosing the right counsellor or therapist

Once clients and counsellors have agreed that a particular sexual problem requires special help they have to decide whether to stay together for treatment or to part in order that the clients should get the kind of help they need.

It is certain that neither counsellors nor therapists are omnipotent or omni-competent, yet it has to be admitted that the therapist is the most important single tool in any healing process, so the choice of the right therapist for a particular situation is important to any client. Clients need to be determined if they want to choose their own therapist. Therapists need to be aware of their own limitations so that if they know that they are unable to help certain individuals they can at least refer them to someone who can.

It should never be regarded as a failure if a counsellor decides that she or he is not the right person to help a particular client or has not the experience or expertise necessary for a special problem. Equally, clients need not feel guilty, though they often do, if they decide that it is time they found someone else to help them. At the same time, once they have committed themselves to therapy with one person, they should not give that therapist up too easily since difficulties in the relationship often point to areas which merit closer attention. Conflicts between clients and therapists can usually be used to facilitate personal growth towards maturity.

The ultimate choice as to whether to stay together or part company should normally remain with the clients. Before they finally commit themselves to a particular therapist or form of therapy they may find it helpful to inquire about their therapist's attitudes towards religious and moral issues. The therapist's opinions will gradually emerge during the course of therapy, although some

130

Freudian analysts could deny this. However, clarification at the outset of a relationship can protect clients and therapists from difficulties and misunderstandings which might otherwise arise at a crucial point during therapy and hinder the healing process. At the beginning of any therapeutic relationship there are some occasions when therapists can disclose their opinions without either over-elaboration or over-simplification. This kind of sharing may confirm the viability of the relationship or expose important flaws and differences of approach which enable clients and therapists to break off their contract before serious difficulties arise.

On the importance of religious and moral attitudes in therapy

Since moral attitudes affect most sexual problems and also many of the types of therapy available for their resolution this is one of the areas of opinion most in need of clarification. Joseph Fletcher has pointed out that,

There are at bottom only three alternative routes or approaches to follow in making moral decisions. They are (1) the legalistic, (2) the antinomian, the opposite extreme—ie a lawless or un-principled approach and (3) the situational.[3]

Apart from psychopaths who have an underdeveloped and/or inappropriate sense of right and wrong, few clients, counsellors or therapists are antinomian. In effect, therefore, clients have to choose between legalists and situational ethicists. As Fletcher says,

The classic role of moral theology has been to follow laws but to do it as much as possible according to love and according to reason (*secundum caritatem et secundum rationem*). Situation ethics on the other hand calls upon us to keep law in a sub-servient phase, so that only love and reason really count when the chips are down.[4]

Fletcher and other like-minded ethicists agree that it is

easier to define law than love. They admit that it is dangerous to say that love (*agapé*) is the only principle (law) that can be applied to every situation regardless of circumstances. Again, it is Fletcher who points out that making decisions based on situation ethics, 'entails a frightful measure of doubt and uncertainty and opacity' but at the same time he challenges his readers to make up their own minds about it when he says: 'We have to decide, to choose whether we lean on law or ride out into the open for love's sake.'[5]

Most people do not really know whether they are legalists or situational ethicists until they are confronted with a moral crisis in their lives, and even then they may believe that they 'fall back on the law' because they are obeying the higher law of love, or they may 'ride out into the open' believing that they are breaking the law for the sake of love. It is only when people look at a number of their important decisions with hindsight that they can see whether they tend more towards legalism or towards empirical solutions which differ in every individual situation.

It is not always safe to assume that a therapist's ethical or philosophical stance corresponds to her or his designated role. Most people, for instance, assume that clergy are legalists, and are surprised to find out that some of them are really situationists. Many people think that analysts are either antinomian or are situational ethicists and they may be astonished to find out that their particular therapists are really legalists at heart. Clients need to find out what their therapists really believe, and therapists certainly need to be able to work within the moral framework which their clients can tolerate if they are to discharge their responsibilities to their clients properly. Failure to establish rapport in this field of human experience has been responsible for a great deal of misunderstanding between therapists and patients to the detriment of both. A brief example will suffice to illustrate some of the difficulties which clients and counsellors may experience at the outset of a relationship.

Simon and Angela believed that their love of God told them to obey the laws of the Church to which they belonged. When Simon unexpectedly fell in love with another person he was dismayed to find out that he could not keep those laws. Angela could not understand his 'moral weakness'. Her judgemental attitude towards him contributed to their eventual separation. But after Simon left she began to suffer from compulsive sexual ruminations. She became ill with anxiety about her own 'moral weakness'. So she sought help from a psychotherapist recommended to her by her family doctor as 'a good Christian'. Angela assumed that he would hold similar views about sex to her own. She was horrified when the psychotherapist suggested that he could think of worse sins than marital infidelity and masturbation.

Angela felt outraged. She brought her therapeutic relationship to an end. She refused all further help, saying that she was never going to risk being told by another psychiatrist to commit sin. She was not able to acknowledge that she might have misinterpreted the psychiatrist's comments, nor was she able to let the 'law of love' move her towards compassion and understanding which might eventually enable her to forgive herself and her husband.

Angela did not succeed in establishing enough rapport with her psychotherapist because she had 'jumped to conclusions' about what he had said. At the same time he may have been premature with his suggestions because he failed to understand what Angela would expect of him as 'a good Christian', and did not, therefore, stay with her feelings for long enough to establish a secure relationship with her before he allowed himself to express his own viewpoint.

People are very sensitive about their religious and moral attitudes towards sexual behaviour. Counsellors and therapists can usually understand enough about their own beliefs to know what guide-lines they normally adopt in their own decision-making processes. They should, therefore, be able to communicate this information to their clients without expecting the latter to agree with them, and without necessarily making definitive statements which might constrict the relationship and prevent it from growing. Therapists should always try to leave their clients sufficient space to be able to expand and mature in their own individual ways.

When those who are beset by sexual problems begin to look for the right person to help them it is vital to remember that the sex of the therapist may be very important in determining the future viability of a therapeutic relationship.

The therapist as a sexual being

Some people believe that the sex of a therapist is irrelevant in any healing relationship. They hold that the knowledge and skill of a therapist can surmount any difficulties which may occur during such an intimate form of treatment. Therapists, after all, are experienced in handling problem relationships. They expect a wide variety of roles to be projected on to them. Male therapists, for instance, are familiar with patients who treat them as if they were mothers, and women therapists know that their clients can adopt them as father figures. When clients project their fantasies on to their therapists the latter can use the difference between fantasy and reality to analyse the 'transference relationship'. Analysts often argue that the analysis of the transference is more important than the sexuality or personality of the therapist.

Others, however, disagree. They do not see the therapist as a blank screen upon which a film is projected so that it can be dissected and analysed by the client with the help of an intelligent expert. These people feel that the sexuality and personality of therapists play an important part in the healing process. Many therapists feel that their own sex is of importance to the establishment of good relations, especially in the early stages where some of the rapport

134

established between therapists and clients depends upon the archetypal roles they both adopt.

Many people also believe that men and women work in fundamentally different ways. They feel that the sex of the therapist is an important factor in any particular therapeutic relationship rather than a coincidental factor of little consequence to the outcome of the therapy. One distinguished family therapist has written:

I have found that men and women are so different in their approach and concept and in their way of working that the mere fact of a woman taking part in a meeting can change the solution of problems in an important way.[6]

Dr Skynner does not describe the differences he observes, however, and while many therapists would intuitively agree with his statement, some would also say that it is very difficult to be certain that one particular way of working is specifically sex linked.

Basic differences between female and male therapists

Attempts to analyse the ways in which female and male therapists differ from each other are usually defeated by a fair-sized minority of the members of one sex capable of displaying the characteristics of the other sex without necessarily losing their identification with their own. Until most people stop thinking of certain personality traits, like gentleness, as feminine, and others, like aggressiveness, as masculine, it will be difficult to identify the difference between women and men without falling into the trap of stereotyping people according to the 'feminine' or masculine' attributes in their personalities and personal behaviour. Even subtle qualities like passivity and activity, which are often thought of as characteristic of women and men respectively, are notoriously difficult to evaluate since many 'feminine' women are actively ambitious in their professional lives and many 'masculine' men are also gentle and receptive at work.

It is important to recognize that there are difficulties in evaluating the differences between female and male therapists. It is particularly difficult to ascertain which observed differences are the result of genetic and hormonal factors and which of childhood 'imprinting' and conditioning. The distinction between nature and nurture is, perhaps, more interesting to academics than to clients, for in the end what matters most to clients are the role differences between female and male therapists. Clients are less interested in how those differences arise than in what those differences mean in terms of their own needs.

Role differences between female and male therapists

Certain observable differences in the roles of women and men therapists can be very useful to clients who know their own needs and who can match their needs with the therapists they choose to help them. Here it is the relationship between role and authority which is important to both clients and therapists.

In the eye of most of their clients male therapists are naturally suited for their work. There is a close correlation between their maleness and their role authority. Clients tend to assume that their male therapists are strong, dominant or even masterful men and they often invest them with parental or conjugal authority. The sexual authority of a male therapist fits in well with his professional role and can be used for the benefit of clients within the expected security of a professional therapeutic relationship. Indeed, there is nothing inherently wrong in a patient's falling in love with a therapist. The adult male therapist who is sexually active, aware and unafraid of his sexuality can help clients of both sexes if he is aware of what he is doing and is in touch with himself. He can make men feel more confident of their manhood by the way he talks to them, touches them and reacts to them. He can also make women feel more loved and appreciated as people in their own right.

In modern western society, men's fears of their own sexuality have lessened. Male therapists are using touch more often than they used to formerly to convey warmth, affection, understanding and admiration. They are more able to express their own fears and feelings. They are less afraid of tears and strong emotions. They are increasingly able to speak frankly about sexual difficulties of their clients. All this is beneficial, and yet the lowering of the invisible but perceptible barriers which exist between therapists and their clients is also dangerous.

When two people are brought together in the intimacy of a therapeutic relationship they may feel such strong sexual attraction for each other that they come to believe that they should consummate their relationship in sexual inter-course. Some therapists act accordingly, but many eminent therapists believe that overt sexual relationships between therapists and clients are destructive to the healing poten-tial of the relationship. Masters and Johnson, for instance, have said: 'There is no greater negation of professional responsibility than taking sexual advantage of an essen-tially defenceless patient; yet this often happens.'[7]

At present there is no adequate information which shows exactly how often therapists do have sexual intercourse with their clients. Masters and Johnson's comment must remain an opinion rather than a statement of fact. It is probable that most therapists and clients do not expect to have sexual intercourse with each other as part of the treat-ment process. Given this limitation, however, a wide variety of sexually based verbal and non-verbal exchanges can take place between male therapists and their male homosexual or female heterosexual clients. Sexual rapport can be an important factor in helping clients to surmount various sexual difficulties, provided that ultimately it leads

137

to the clients' independence or interdependence rather than to an unhealthy dependence on their therapists.

Women therapists, on the other hand, experience more difficulty in using their own sexuality in therapy. In their professional roles women are expected to be able to take the initiative in establishing and maintaining creative relationships with their clients; yet in their private lives heterosexual women are still expected to be receptive of attention rather than active in pursuit. Women's professional roles are, therefore, to some extent at variance with their domestic and social roles.

This contradiction of sexual roles may not be recognized by therapists or their clients, but it often exists, and it sometimes induces women therapists to take the initiative through the less overtly sexual approach of the maternal role. This approach is generally acceptable to clients. Women's professional role-authority harmonizes with their maternal role, so women therapists are usually expected to speak to and touch their clients as if they were mothers or even elder sisters. In this role they can parallel and complement their male colleagues who are acting as fathers and brothers to their clients, but it is not at all easy for women to parallel the husband role. They cannot make overt sexual advances to their clients unless they are willing to risk being gravely misunderstood, even though it is true that sexual relationships between women and men are undergoing radical changes in modern society.

Women therapists are, therefore, at some disadvantage compared with their male colleagues. A man, for instance, can easily indicate that he finds some of his patients to be sexually attractive by the way in which he approaches them. A woman cannot so easily make advances to her clients without arousing some role-confusion. The small gestures and signals which women use socially to indicate their willingness to be approached by potential sexual partners are not so easy to use unself-consciously in a woman doctor/client situation. In western society, where sexual roles still play an important part in courtship, this lack of correspondence between professional and social roles can mean that it can be difficult for a woman therapist to make her clients feel better by indicating that she finds them sexually attractive even though she has no intention of inviting them to have sexual intercourse with her.

Women therapists cannot so easily retain their professional role-authority and remain sexually attractive, and this apparent discrepancy can account for some of the initial dislike which many people feel when they meet dominant women in positions of authority, or when they try to relate to women therapists. Nevertheless, within the last two decades, there have been considerable changes in people's attitudes towards professional women, and women therapists are learning to overcome their handicaps so that they can use their sexuality to help their clients.

Parental and friendship roles

Those clients who need their therapists to be strong authority figures, at any rate initially, undoubtedly find it helpful to ask for advice from men and women who are secure in their parental authority roles, or who are confident enough about their sexuality to make good use of it. If the treatment is continued for long enough, and in such a manner that it has a good chance of being successful, the initial relationship between therapists and clients will change and develop as the clients mature and their therapists hand back some of their parental responsibility to them.

Some potential clients are deterred from seeking help because they are afraid that parental or authority figures can so easily become authoritarian through faults either in the therapists or in their clients. Some of these people, together with others who have never had any need for parental replacement figures, do very well with non-directive therapists. They are likely to seek out therapists who adopt sibling roles in preference to parental ones, or who see themselves as skilled friends rather than as healing experts. Women are well suited to this kind of non-directive, non-authoritarian, therapeutic relationship since its gentle approach fits in well with the general public's image of a female way of working. Prospective clients may find themselves attracted to women therapists, and/or gentle men for this reason.

All the same those who look to non-authoritarian figures to help them in their search for wholeness need to be able to recognize the difference between softness and gentleness. Although they may find the early stages of therapy more helpful if they do not encounter rigid parental or authoritarian attitudes in their therapists, they will not be helped as much by therapists who are too soft to assume parental responsibility when necessary as by those who are willing to help their clients to face up to the hard facts of life, and the difficult choices which must be made from time to time. If they are fortunate, clients who go to gentle therapists of either sex will, at some time, encounter in their therapists a rock-hard firmness challenging them to make effective choices to take them in the direction of renewal and health.

Finding the right treatment

There are now so many different treatments available for the cure of sexual disorders that it is often difficult for clients to know which to choose and to discover where the treatment of their choice might be available.

It is, unfortunately, all too easy for therapists to assume that they will automatically choose the right type of treatment for each of their clients because of their knowledge about, and experience in, sexual therapy. So they tend to make their own decisions and then they communicate them to their clients in such a way that it is difficult for the clients to refuse the proffered advice. Most therapists assume that their clients retain their freedom to stop therapy whenever they want to, but it is not at all easy for people to renounce a helping hand at the very moment when they feel they are drowning, so this option is a theoretical rather than a real one.

If therapists and clients can avoid slipping into this trap of the expert automatically assuming power over the client at the very outset of the relationship, their partnership will start off on a different basis altogether. When clients can join their therapists in choosing the type of treatment they need they have a better chance of staying together when the relationship comes under strain. Clients who trust their therapists because they fully understand the nature of their treatment, and are willing to undergo some hardship for the sake of their eventual cure, are less likely to panic when they have to experience some suffering during the course of their treatment.

All this may sound very obvious and, indeed, it should be, but unfortunately it is, for instance, still quite usual to find clients who are having behaviour therapy without really understanding that they cannot get better without enduring some painful feelings during their progress towards health. While it is possible that adequate explanations have been misunderstood, it is surely important for bewildered clients to be able to share their anxieties with their therapists by asking them questions; yet, in practice, clients often return to their family doctors instead to ask their questions and voice their concern, or they drop out of therapy altogether because they cannot understand what is happening to them. It is, therefore, necessary for therapists to remind themselves of the importance of their clients' being able to participate in the decisions that are being made all the time about their treatment. Clients need to be given sufficient opportunity to ask all the questions they want to about their treatment throughout its progress.

It is never too easy to arrive at the initial and vital decisions about the best course of treatment for a particular sexual problem because so much of the outcome of any therapy depends upon the clients' personalities and their interactions with their relatives, friends and therapists. It seems sensible, therefore, to list some of the treatments that are often recommended to clients whose problems are not yielding to counselling. These treatments are available from individual therapists, from two co-therapists, usually of different sexes, or from small groups of other clients under the overall guidance of one or more therapists.

Behaviour therapy

Behaviour therapy is designed to modify undesirable patterns of bodily response to normal events in a person's life. It is, for instance, often used in the treatment of phobias where a normal event, like going out of doors or getting on to a bus, will precipitate an acute fear reaction which is out of all proportion to the proposed activity. Phobias are common, and they cause great misery to their victims. Phobic people know how stupid it is for them to be afraid but they are quite unable to control their inappropriate fear. Phobia is an extreme form of anxiety, and anxiety is very common among people with sexual problems, so behaviour therapy is popular treatment for sexual disorders like impotence and premature ejaculation, when these are due to anxiety. It can also be used to help some women who experience pain and vaginal spasm when they attempt to have sexual intercourse.

During behaviour therapy clients are often given tranquillizers, either orally, or by intramuscular or intravenous injection. They are then encouraged to imagine the feared sexual situation in the presence of, and with the psychological support of, the therapist. The use of drugs can be, and is often, reduced by teaching clients simple relaxation exercises which they can practise in preparation for their therapy session. With appropriate training and encouragement clients can learn, first to tolerate their anxiety, then to control it, and finally to exchange their anxious reactions to given sexual stimuli for pleasurable ones to the same stimuli.

Treatment programmes generally last from six to twelve weeks and the clients' sexual partners are expected to be actively involved in the therapy. The partners' help is very important to the success of some special types of behaviour therapy like the Masters and Johnson technique.

The Masters and Johnson technique and modifications
The Masters and Johnson technique, and all its many modifications which are currently in use for helping people with sexual dysfunctions, depends upon being able to reduce anxiety while at the same time increasing sexual pleasure. The couple, who have developed crippling anxieties in relation to the sexual relationship between them, are asked to relate to each other sensually rather than sexually. They are told to practise relaxation exercises together and to give one another sensual pleasure through touching, stroking or massaging areas of each other's body which have hitherto been neglected because of the partner's repeated struggles to accomplish successful sexual intercourse.

During this stage of the training the couple are specifically forbidden to make any attempt to reproduce the sexual behaviour which brought on their problem. So, for instance, if a man complains of premature ejaculation he and his partner are forbidden to attempt sexual intercourse. Instead, each partner is asked to discover the other's sensual pleasure zones and to fondle one another to the point of pleasure but not sexual arousal. Once the client has learned to relax and enjoy his sensations of pleasure he is allowed to go on to sexual arousal provided it does not precipitate undue anxiety or orgasm. If he knows that he is not going to be asked to risk a premature ejaculation inside his partner's body he can enjoy himself and in time can train his body to prolong that enjoyment rather than terminate it precipitately.

143

This kind of treatment, which aims to teach people to observe their own emotional reactions, is called 'sensate focus training', or 'passive concentration training'. It persuades people to make a mental note of the pleasure they are experiencing and to link that pleasure with the sexual arousal they begin to feel. Once this link is well established the natural sexual mechanisms of the body can take over. This method is different from trying to achieve success by insisting that clients should force their bodies to respond to sexual stimuli when these are being contradicted by strong feelings of anxiety or repugnance.

Premature ejaculation has been cited only as one example of the way in which behaviour therapy can be used for the treatment of sexual disorders where the problem is complicated by anxiety. The technique is also useful in a wide variety of other sexual dysfunctions, including frigidity, dyspareunia and some kinds of male impotence.

Behaviour therapy is often used in conjunction with other forms of treatment. Women, for instance, who have difficulty in reaching orgasm with a sexual partner can sometimes be helped by learning to achieve orgasm with the help of a mechanical vibrator. Similarly, some impotent men can be helped by a variety of mechanical aids some of which are referred to in a later section of this chapter. The best-known adjunct to behaviour therapy, however, is the use of the 'Seman's grip' for the treatment of premature ejaculation, where, at the point just before ejaculation, the glans of the penis is gripped by the man's partner between the thumb, placed on the frenulum underneath the penis, and the two forefingers placed on the corona on the upper side of the penis. The penis is squeezed firmly for about ten seconds and this will usually avert a premature ejaculation. The procedure is repeated as often as necessary and in time the client learns to hold back until he and his partner are ready for orgasm.

Behavioural therapy is an excellent form of treatment for the right conditions and in the right hands. It does, however, make considerable demands on clients. They have to be self-disciplined and trustful enough to follow the advice of their therapist if they are to regain their health. Unfortunately, some people are unable to profit from behaviour therapy, either because they lack the ability to be patient with themselves or they cannot accept help from other people. They tend to blame their therapists and to complain about the stupidity of the treatment regimes rather than to question their own responsibility for their failure to recover. If they can be persuaded to 'try again' they often do much better on the second occasion.

Behaviour therapy is not a panacea. Its more negative forms like aversion therapy have not been outstandingly successful in the treatments of sexual maladjustment. It is now generally recognized that aversion therapy is useless for changing true heterosexuals into homosexuals, or vice versa, although it is still recommended for helping some bisexuals, transvestites and fetishists who want to reorientate. Bisexuals, for instance, who desperately want to become homosexual or heterosexual can be turned away from their disliked orientation by aversion therapy, using painful electric shocks or emetic drugs to inhibit the unwanted sexual arousal, but the effect of this treatment is seldom permanent. It has to be reinforced by further treatment. Such therapy is time consuming and it cannot guarantee that clients will find any increased pleasure with the sexual partners of their choice. Indeed, aversion therapy sometimes leaves clients worse off than they were before, for once they have learnt to dislike one type of sexual behaviour they may find themselves repelled by all sexual activity. In the end they may become unable to enjoy any sexual arousal.

Behaviour therapy may need to be complemented or replaced by other forms of treatment, of which psychotherapy remains the best known.

Psychotherapy in all its various forms aims to help clients to explore their present difficulties in relation to their past experiences, particularly those of early childhood, in the hope that, by uncovering the sources of their distress and understanding themselves better, clients will be able to modify their attitudes and behaviour at will.

Orthodox Freudian, Jungian or Adlerian psychoanalysis on an individual basis is a costly and time-consuming process, so only a few privileged people can afford to pay for therapy which will involve their seeing an analyst three or four times a week. This harsh reality has forced many analytically minded therapists and clients to look for other ways of putting their analytic principles into practice. There have been some interesting developments in therapy as a result of this search for other methods. Clients, for instance, who started off with an individual analyst, might find themselves transferred into small groups of people sharing one analyst between several of them, because they could not afford the luxury of a personal analyst. Some of them have discovered that this group method has had distinct advantages over the individual consultation, for they have been greatly helped by their colleagues in the group as well as by the analyst.

When people join psychotherapy groups once or twice a week over a fairly long period of time they have many opportunities of seeing themselves as other people see them. They discover that other people pick up information about them that they had thought they kept secret, or that they did not even realize was part of their personality. They also discover that they can interpret the words and actions of other members of the group in ways which can be very helpful in a group setting. This ability to be healed by others, and to heal them in turn, has led to a rediscovery of self-help methods of therapy, and to a recovery of self-confidence among those who have sexual problems and who want to cope with them with only a modicum of paid professional help.

It is well known that therapists are divided among themselves as to whether psychotherapy is more or less effective than behaviour therapy as a technique for dealing with sexual problems. The limited statistics which are available indicate that they are equally good or equally bad, depending upon whether the assessors are optimists or pessimists. Individual results depend largely upon the particular needs of clients, and the way in which those needs are met by therapy, so decisions about which form of treatment to adopt are usually a matter of personal preference. It has to be admitted, however, that it is generally more difficult to assess the progress of psychotherapy than that of behaviour therapy simply because feelings are less tangible and measurable than behaviour patterns.

Treatment by psychotherapy can tend to meander on for many months or even years without appreciable improvement. Attempts have been made to reduce the chances of this happening by arranging that contracts are made between therapists and clients for a limited period of treatment after which the therapy can be terminated or a new contract negotiated. Some clients and therapists certainly work better when they are under the moderate pressure of a time-limited contract, and many of them benefit from periodic reviews of the problems which brought them together in the first place.

In recent years considerable attention has been paid to helping therapists to become more sensitive to the dynamics of their consultations and to the nuances of clients' behaviour during the treatment sessions. It has been realized that a great deal can be done for people through a limited series of short interviews provided that clients and therapists co-operate well and work hard within this framework. This sensitivity training of therapists in Balint-type seminars (so called after Dr Balint, a psycho-analyst who started seminar training for a group of family doctors in the late 1940s), and, more recently, in psycho-sexual seminars, organized for the Family Planning Association by Dr Tom Main and his colleagues at the Cassel Hospital, has extended many of the benefits of psychotherapy to people who would not otherwise be able to take advantage of formal individual or group psychoanalytic therapy. By training a large number of family doctors, social workers, marriage-guidance counsellors and family planning personnel a larger number of clients can be reached than would be possible if the trainers were to by-pass the primary health care team and offer their skills directly to patients. Similar ideas have been responsible for the emergence of highly professional training schemes such as those offered by the Westminster Pastoral Foundation and the Clinical Theology Association (*see* Appendix C).

Hormone and drug therapy

Most people think of sexual intercourse as a pleasant activity as well as a procreative duty. Throughout recorded history, therefore, men and women have tried to heighten sexual pleasure, to prolong its duration or to restore lost libido by using aphrodisiacs and other drugs which can enhance a person's sexual performance.

People's identities are intimately linked to their self-esteem which is also directly affected by their own and other people's estimations of their sexual performance and potency.

The male hormone, *testosterone*, is widely used for the treatment of male impotence. It can be given sublingually, orally, by injection or implant and it is effective in those who are deficient in this hormone. It is also often used for the treatment of menopausal or post-menopausal women whose sexual desires have waned with their advancing years. Its use may be accompanied by unpleasant side effects like headaches and general impairment of fertility in men, and acne and hirsute conditions in women.

The fertility drug, *bromocriptene*, which is widely used to help women with anovular menstrual cycles to produce eggs so that they can become pregnant, can also help a small number of men whose impotence is due to the rare condition of hyperprolactinaemia.

Hormone replacement therapy

Conjugated oestrogens like *premarin*, *provera* and *harmogen* are known to benefit many menopausal women. They may improve their sense of well-being and libido. Hormone replacement therapy has become fashionable, but its undoubted advantages in prolonging women's youthful appearance and delaying the onset of diseases associated with ageing, such as painful osteoporosis of the bones and coronary artery disease, have to be weighed against some disadvantages. Women on some forms of hormone replacement therapy, for instance, are more liable than other post-menopausal women to develop sudden complications because of wandering blood clots in their circulation. All women on hormone replacement therapy should be carefully screened at regular intervals, but those women who still have an intact uterus need special screening because they are more likely than other women to develop cancer of the body of the uterus. There is not enough known as yet about the long-term effects of hormone therapy to justify the extravagant claims that are sometimes made on its behalf.

The majority of people who need hormone therapy for sexual disorders are afflicted by a diminution or inhibition of sexual desire and performance. There are, however, a number of people who seem to be too highly sexed. They have problems because their sexual arousal systems respond more quickly and easily than the average person's, or because they are aroused by unusual stimuli which do not appeal to most people.

Hormones and chemical inhibitors

Certain drugs are well known to depress libido and they have often been used to help people to control or damp down their sexual arousal systems without making them impotent. *Stilboestrol*, for instance, has been used to help some men who suffer from unacceptable sexual desires which they cannot control by will power or behavioural conditioning techniques. In recent years a very effective drug, *androcur*, has been discovered. It can help men who have committed sexual crimes to control their unlawful impulses. This drug, however, virtually castrates men, and the ethical problems surrounding its use have not yet been satisfactorily resolved.

It is also known that some types of contraceptive pills can depress the female libido and so some women have asked for them to help them to control their masturbatory fantasies or nymphomaniac tendencies.

Hormones are useful in the treatment of many sexual disorders, but there are other agents which can be just as helpful. Tranquillizers and certain drugs known as beta-blockers, like *oxyprenol (trasicor)*, are sometimes used to alleviate anxiety or muscular incoordination which threatens to ruin a potentially good relationship because of the excessive resistence of one or both partners whenever the act of sexual intercourse is attempted.

Drugs like cannabis, alcohol and L.S.D. have been widely used as aphrodisiacs, but they appear to have more effect on the imagination than on performance. It is relatively common to hear a heavy social drinker boasting about his sexual prowess when he has drunk his fill at the pub with 'the boys' while his sexual partners wink their dissent in the background.

Hormones and drugs undoubtedly having a valuable part to play in the treatment of people with sexual malfunctions. They are a useful adjunct to the ministrations of experienced counsellors or therapists, but can seldom replace personal help in such a sensitive area of life. Unfortunately many clients with sexual problems are very shy about discussing their intimate affairs with other people, with the result that many of them find it difficult to get the help they so badly need.

Some of these potential clients turn instead to the 'agony columns' of newspapers for advice or use the 'phone-in' couselling services which are a feature of some radio programmes. Those who run these community-based services are often very helpful to shy inquirers and they can do a great deal to help clients to take the initiative in seeking more personal contacts with other helping agencies. Some people, however, cannot bring themselves to write or phone in order to get help. They may turn instead to books about sexual behaviour and sexual intercourse in an attempt to help themselves.

Self help and sex aids
Many people in society are still very ignorant about sexual matters, so responsible books, films and videotapes can break down some of this ignorance, combat some prejudices and help people to discover that many of their own sexual patterns of behaviour are shared by other people, and are either within normal limits or can be helped by relatively simple means. Shy people can often be helped by explicit literature and films about sexual behaviour: even those who have the courage to seek personal help can profit from books and visual aids; so it is important for counsellors and therapists to be able to recommend suitable material to their clients (*see* Appendix C: Useful Books and Contacts).

Therapists are so used to talking about other people's sexual reactions and difficulties that they often ignore their own or even deny that they are capable of sudden and unexpectedly powerful sexual reactions to unusual or unfamiliar sexual stimuli. Professional sex therapists can become insensitive to their clients' feelings and needs unless they are in touch with their own, so they need to take care not to be cynical about their own capacity for sexual pleasure and pain. Erotic books and films can help some of them to remain in touch with a wide range of emotions even when their own physical experience is limited by personal circumstances.

The use of sex aids like vibrators and coronal rings, to overcome sexual dysfunctions and to enhance sexual pleasure is gaining ground as more people lose their inhibitions about sexual experience.

Mechanical aids have been suspect largely because some of them, like Blakoe energizing rings or battery-operated clitoral vibrators, seem to contradict the idea that sexual pleasure is only truly fulfilling if it is the expression of two people's mutual love for each other. Some people enjoy sexual stimulation by mechanical sexual aids more than the touch of their lovers, and it would appear that some of those who object to their use fear that many people might become so dependent on their aids and so self-sufficient that they could dispense with intimate human relationship altogether. While this may happen to a tiny number of men and women the great majority of people use sex aids only to help themselves to establish better sexual relationships with those whom they love. Sometimes these mechanical aids enable people to experience orgasm for the first time in their lives or to recover this experience after a long period of anxiety over sexual dysfunction. The Blakoe energizing ring, for instance, which encircles the penis and testicles, produces slight engorgement of the sexual organs through restricting the venous blood return. It may enable older men who suffer from erectile difficulties to regain some of their former ability to achieve sexual penetration and to have a satisfying orgasm.

Men who use mechanical aids may regain their sexual confidence and potency and then be able to do without the mechanical help. Similarly, a woman who has difficulty in reaching a sexual climax can be helped to reach orgasm if the man wears a coronal ring during sexual intercourse. This is a rubber ring which is covered by soft fronds which create a pleasurable friction inside the vagina. Patterned and rugose condoms, sometimes known as 'French ticklers', fulfil the same purpose, but they are not safe to use as contraceptives. Some women, especially those who have seriously handicapped sexual partners, or who are on their own, use vibrators and dildos with pleasure.

Those who work with people with psychosexual problems know that sexual aids may speed up their clients' progress towards health if they are given a chance and are used sensibly and sensitively. Unfortunately there is still widespread ignorance about the proper use of sex aids and many people in western society seem to associate them with pornography rather than with therapy and healthy sexual intercourse.

Those who are concerned with sex education need to identify and clarify the differences between healthy interest, therapy and pornography so that sex shops, film producers and publishers can offer a wide range of interesting educational material without recourse to unpleasant 'soft' or 'hard' pornography or making use of children. This is an urgent task confronting western society which individuals must take seriously if the association between sex and violence is to be curtailed for the good of the whole community.

Surrogate therapy
The use of surrogate partners in sex therapy has always been controversial, largely because surrogates are widely regarded as prostitutes rather than as therapists in their own right who have a specialized knowledge about a particular sphere of sexual activity. It is true that sensitive prostitutes can also be good surrogate therapists. The main difference between them is that prostitutes are chosen directly by their clients, whereas surrogates are selected

by the sexual therapists who are responsible for their client's treatment.

Counsellors and clients, whatever their religious and moral attitudes, have to consider the possibility of surrogate therapy in cases where the problem cannot be resolved by any other means. Peter's problem illustrates their dilemma.

Peter was a young man who made friends easily. He never had any trouble inviting women friends to go out with him and he enjoyed their company. He had always known that his penis was on the small side compared with other men of his age, but he had enjoyed masturbation as much as the other boys at school so its size did not worry him very much. So Peter was quite confident on the day that he decided to have sexual intercourse with a steady girl friend whom he thought he might eventually marry. She evidently had more experience than he for she laughed at him and taunted him about his 'half-sized cock'. They broke off their relationship at once, but by the time Peter had recovered his morale sufficiently to attempt intercourse again he was already tense before he began. He managed to penetrate his partner but then felt his penis go flaccid. It stayed that way.

After four disastrous attempts at intercourse Peter's morale was broken. He could still enjoy self-stimulation but he knew that it was going to be useless to try to make love to another person. So he went to a psychotherapist for a few months and he had some modified behaviour therapy, but as he had no steady girl friend the best kind of help was not available to him. Drug therapy proved useless in his case and after a while both he and his therapist felt that he would be able to learn how to relax and enjoy sexual intercourse only if he could be taught to do so by an understanding woman who would neither ridicule him if he failed to maintain an erection nor discourage him from trying again. When the therapist suggested introducing him to a surrogate partner he found himself in a moral quandary. As a Christian he wanted to live up to the ideals of his faith. He knew that trying to have intercourse before marriage fell short of the ideal but by now he also knew that his self-confidence was so damaged by his unhappy experience that he was not able to form any close relationships at all. He was convinced that it would be wrong for him to marry anyone in the hope that 'it would be all right on the night'.

Peter took his problem to a priest who told him that in this instance his only possible course of action was to opt for the least of all evils open to him. Together they looked at the options. Peter could choose to accept the loneliness of permanent sexual impotence. He could deliberately form a relationship with a woman and marry her knowing that he might not be able to consummate the marriage. He could go on charming his girl friends into allowing him to make use of their bodies until he found one who was willing to help him to be healed. He could face his problem honestly and pay for the help he needed.

In the end Peter chose the last of these options. He was greatly helped by a skilled woman who was slightly older than he. His self-confidence returned. He was able to form a loving relationship with a girl friend and they eventually married.

Some Christians might have preferred the option of celibacy as the least of all evils or the best of all possible choices in this situation, but Peter did not feel that this would have been a free-will choice for him since he was bound to celibacy by his sexual dysfunction and so was not really free to renounce what he did not fully possess. These kinds of choice are never easy to make but they have to be made even when the ultimate selection turns out to be the refusal to choose.

It is obviously easier to recommend surrogate therapy to single men and women, but some therapists offer it to people who are quite unable to relate to their partners, even though they love them deeply and want to form good sexual relationships with them. Their anxiety may be the factor which prevents them from being able to function adequately, and a surrogate may be able to break that vicious circle simply because there is no powerful emotion of love between surrogate and client. Surrogate therapy for married people, or anyone who is in a relationship with another, undoubtedly entails taking risks and those risks are justifiable only when every other course of action has failed and both partners consent to try surrogate therapy because it offers them their only real chance of success.

Friendship therapy

Friendship is a creative relationship. Friends are able to trust each other, and they enjoy each other's company. Friendship can flourish between people of different temperaments and it can survive differences of opinion, arguments and wars. It is a relationship of loyalty even when physical separation makes contact difficult or impossible.

Friendship is a secure relationship. Women and men who need sexual counselling certainly need that kind of security. Unfortunately, many people who have sexual problems cut themselves off from true friendship because they are ashamed of themselves. They avoid the intimacy which is part of any deep friendship because they are afraid that they will find themselves making a confession about their secret difficulties to someone whose good opinion they value too much to risk losing. So they deny themselves the chance of the help they so badly need.

Some people do not find it easy to make friends because they cannot get past the initial stages of an acquaintanceship to form the closer relationship of friendship. Instead they attempt to win friends for themselves through making overt gestures of affection and sexual interest. When they do this prematurely they introduce an element of insecurity into the relationship which it may not be able to bear. The person to whom the sexual advance or offer is made may not yet be sure enough of the feelings generated by the relationship to know whether or not the suggestion of sexual intimacy is a way of avoiding friendship or of deepening it.

Clients who are in perpetual trouble with their personal relationships, who form passionate unions for short periods and then find themselves mysteriously abandoned, who cannot avoid stormy arguments with people they consider to be their friends, who are constantly demanding more from their friends than the friends are prepared to give, may need to learn what real friendship can be like from counsellors who are willing to offer that kind of a relationship to some clients.

Counsellors sometimes say that they feel sorry that some people are so lonely and friendless that they are willing to buy time with a professional person as a substitute for unsolicited friendship. Some counsellors also admit that although their clients consider them to be their friends, they do not reciprocate the feeling because they would never willingly meet their clients socially. Other counsellors believe that it is only by making friendships with clients that the clients can have any chance of experiencing the delights of true friendship, and the incentive to work at making new friends outside the therapeutic situation.

This is an area of client/counsellor relations which is fraught with difficulties because the relationship may have to be limited by factors like time, availability and economic considerations. Counsellors and therapists can make relatively few friends in this way and they are bound to be selective in choosing friends from among their clients.

Healing friendships are different from formal professional relationships since they are more like the relationship between Samaritan befrienders and clients, priests and parishoners, or spiritual directors and those who call them their 'soul friends'.

The client/counsellor healing friendship offers clients a creative relationship within certain parameters which offer security and stability. The counsellor brings to the friendship certain skills, continuity of interest, loyalty, the willingness to speak the truth in love, the acceptance of distorted and possibly immature feelings from the client. A counsellor who agrees to befriend clients must be willing to accept help and signs of affection from them. The client offers to the relationship as much openness and self-expression as possible. He or she tries to listen to the truth and to react to it in ways which will result in a change of attitude and behaviour. A client will usually find something to offer to the counsellor, even those who are professional, which the counsellor or therapist needs. When clients and counsellors share such good intentions they create a climate in which their friendship can grow.

In this author's opinion a healing friendship should always include a definite commitment to abstain from sexual intercourse with each other, at any rate during the period of the therapy. Such an agreement can offer them both a security which may be very important to the continuance of their relationship. It is one of the reasons why men and women under religious vows make such good friends. Their vow sets limits which are an important factor in such a secure friendship. Happily married people who consider their marriage vow to be binding bring the same quality to their friendships. It has to be said that the author's point of view is not shared by all those who are willing to make friends with some of their clients. Some counsellors and therapists imply that they do sometimes have sexual intercourse with their clients. They say that their method works well but as most of them are reluctant to discuss their work openly it is impossible to test the evidence properly.

In practice the decision not to have extra-marital sexual intercourse with friends simplifies life greatly, since many problems can be avoided by this stance, and, as far as professional relationships are concerned, such a decision provides a great deal of security to those who decide to extend their counselling practice beyond their consulting rooms.

Therapeutic friendships are less successful in formal settings of hospital or consulting rooms with white-coated doctors, desks and uniformed nurse-chaperones than in more informal surroundings where people can relate to each other through shared work-tasks and at social functions. That is why many psychiatric hospitals have allowed nurses to wear their own clothes rather than uniforms when they are on duty. Many have encouraged some blurring of roles so that doctors, nurses, social workers, ward orderlies and cleaners can all interact with their clients in a friendly way while offering them an expertise which is available whenever it is needed.

Hospitals, nevertheless, are structured institutions, so when clients are well enough to leave they are often offered further treatment at a day hospital where the structure can be even less obvious. Private practitioners who make friends with their clients will find themselves eating meals with them, meeting them socially, working together and receiving a great deal from their clients in the process.

It is certainly risky to mix professional help with friendship, and this kind of therapy, creative as it is, is most easily undertaken by counsellors who are well accustomed to living with whirling emotions for they will certainly find themselves sucked into the turbulence of their clients' lives. The counsellors and therapists who are most successful in using friendship as a therapy are those who have simple needs, simple desires, a measure of self-discipline and who have already shown themselves to be capable of making and keeping friends outside their professional environments. They understand how to cope with the strains that come to nearly all friendships. They are able to help their clients to discover how to make and keep other friends. When clients' lives are enriched in this way they can become more self-confident and less dependent on their friendships with their counsellors, while at the same time they are able to retain a link with a valuable relationship.

It is difficult to be dispassionate about sex therapy. Those who undertake such delicate work know that it is always difficult to be sure that the best possible therapy is available to clients.[8] Moreover, ethical problems nearly always complicate the treatment and at times hinder its progress. Human beings are moral beings and true health cannot be bought at the expense of moral integrity. It is only through striving to realize their ideals that people discover the reality of themselves and can learn to accept both their limitations and their potential for wholeness. So it is important to look at some of the ways in which human beings express their sexual ideals through their attempts to use their sexuality in creative ways.

SIX

Creative Sex

Counsellors spend so much of their time trying to help people that they sometimes forget that sex and sexuality are generally taken for granted, that sexual desire is the source of excitement and ecstasy for most people, and that it can lead to the most intimate and fulfilling loving relationships in human experience.

Sex enriches people's lives. Their biological sex and gender colours their individual existences and determines the quality of their relationships. Their sexual orientation energizes their interactions with other people. Sexual desire prompts women and men towards a search for fulfilment through a variety of rich relationships. It prompts some people to remain celibate. It enables others to move towards the creative intimacy of sexual intercourse with beloved partners. It attracts some people towards parenthood. It cements the partnership between two people and enables them to bring new life into the world. The drive towards procreation helps parents to nourish and protect their children until they grow to maturity.

The sexual drive does not necessarily find its outlet in sexual intercourse. Some people remain virgin or celibate by choice. Some enjoy their sexuality through their non-genital friendships. Some people channel some of their sexual energy into creative activities like worship, drama, art, writing and various kinds of pastoral care. Great unhappiness or illness may diminish the sexual drive, but this drive will be stronger in the long run than the adverse influences caused by temporary setbacks, and the desire for genital intimacy will then reassert itself.

Creative sexuality has a visible and tangible beauty about it which is very attractive. Love is the source of all creative sexuality, and the ability to love and be loved is an ideal to which most people aspire, even when they know that they are incapable of living close to that ideal. It is possible to see this creative sexuality at work in every kind of person and relationship, but it is most easily visible in certain ways of living.

Virginity and celibacy

Virginity and celibacy can be destructive or creative ways of life. In their destructive aspects they can be responsible for turning men and women into shrivelled caricatures of themselves. In their creative aspects they can impart a luminous quality to people's lives which is most attractive.

When men and women choose to remain virgin or become celibates they expect to use their sexual energies in ways different from the more usual ones of forming genital relationships. Many of these single people who live alone or in community, as, for instance, do nuns and monks, are warm, loving people. They do not see themselves as frustrated spinsters and bachelors. They do not try to deny the existence of their sexual drives. Instead they try to use them creatively as they channel them into the work which they undertake for the sake of, and in the name of Love. Moreover, they expect their work to bear fruit. They will not bear children, but they do 'give birth' to new ideas, new relationships, new organizations. These single people, whether they live alone or in community, are neither more nor less virtuous than those who are married or living with sexual partners, but they have a freedom of movement and action which is seldom so readily available to those with family and partnership commitments. This freedom is not only confined to those who have chosen virginity or celibacy as a way of life, but it is also available to all those who find themselves saddled with enforced celibacy and then decide to use it creatively. In her book, *Who Walk Alone*, Margaret Evening, herself a celibate, illustrates the advantages she sees in this freedom of celibacy. She says:

The possibilities for exploring love within that freedom are endless and exciting. Moreover, the creative urge which is in all of us may still produce its offspring even though they may not be of flesh and blood. History will demonstrate how often a particular establishment, movement, cause or monument has been 'conceived' and carried by those who are single till, in time, they bring it forth as a gift to the world.[1]

It is easy to see the truth of this statement in the lives of people like Mother Teresa of Calcutta and Roger Schutz of Taizé, but it is even more important to discern it in the lives of the Little Sisters of Jesus down the road, the single school teacher, the elderly widow next door. Another writer, Gilbert Russell, captures the ordinariness of this beauty when he says:

The three great ends of marriage hold good ... in the deepest sense, not only for husbands and wives but for single persons as well. They also can be united in affection and common life, with another or more than one. They can 'reproduce themselves' in a host of creative ways, in work and friendship and service to other folk. What they give to the world is often more precious than sons. The fabric of civilization could not have been reared without them, and could hardly be maintained. Their gifts to mankind may endure beyond any posterity. Their 'society' gladdens and they bless with their 'help and comfort' uncounted men and women. We have all rejoiced in the friendship of people like this. 'Frustration' is a word which dies in their company.[2]

Few people are called to celibacy for life, but most people have spells of involuntary celibacy to face and it is during these times that the example of the voluntary celibates can be so helpful, for their lives make it obvious that it is possible to live happy and fruitful celibate lives without coming to any harm. People who feel that life has come to an end if they cannot have sexual intercourse for some reason can be helped to come to terms with their own situation if they can see celibacy as a creative possibility rather than as a destructive consequence of disastrous proportions.

The lives of people who are able to use celibacy creatively can also inspire and encourage men and women who are living in partnership where genital sexual intimacy forms part of a loving relationship, for celibates often know how to be chaste, and chastity is a virtue that is visibly creative in the lives of celibates and sexually active people alike.

Chastity

A Christian writer, Donald Goergen, has pointed out that:

Chastity is that virtue which integrates the totality of sexuality into our lives as Christian men and women, which strives to unify the sexual and spiritual dimensions of a person, whether single or married, which universalizes affectivity in the direction of compassion and sees genitality as a sign of God's love for men by limiting it to a faithful and sustained commitment.[3]

Christians cannot expect to have a monopoly on virtue and so that definition must surely apply to men and women who are not Christian as well as to Christians. It is positive in its affirmation that chastity is not an enemy of sexuality but a friend. It serves humanity by integrating people's sexuality into their total personalities.

Chastity is an elusive virtue. It often communicates itself to others in a subtle way. They get an intuitive feeling that chaste people are so collected inside themselves that they can be trusted to be in control of their affections and emotions. At the same time truly chaste people are always vulnerable, open to others, able to give and receive love. They are also able to make other people feel lovable.

Chaste people are often put to the test. Their friends and enemies alike sense the ambiguity of their position and want to know whether or not they can be seduced from their single-mindedness. The challengers do not necessarily wish to gain the victory over a chaste person, but at the same time will often be prepared to take advantage of the situation if they see any sign of a weakening of intention. The ability to refuse even powerful seduction adds strength to the beauty and attractiveness of the virtue of chastity.

Once people have been able to experience the pleasure of being able to feel deep love and affection for other people without having to gratify their own self-centred needs, they can begin to enjoy being chaste without having their joy spoilt by the complicated emotion of guilt. Just as great athletes win applause from spectators who appreciate the disciplined hard work lying behind their performance, so chaste people command admiration because they are in control of themselves. Their chastity wins its own reward and their increased self-esteem helps them to remain chaste.

Chastity can be presented in an attractive way to clients with sexual problems and many of them are very willing to work hard in order to acquire this virtue because they understand the connection between chastity and love, and they believe that when they are able to be chaste they will also be able to get closer to their ideal of being able to love and be loved.

The ability to be chaste does not come about through dogged determination and heroic endeavour to adopt self-restraint as a way of life. People who keep tight reins on their own sexual drives usually succeed only in controlling their energies, not in releasing them to be fully used in the creative relationships of love. The ability to be chaste and, therefore, able to love and be loved without fear of using one's sexuality to destroy other people's relationships depends upon an understanding of sexuality that enables one to consider other people's needs in relation to one's own personal needs.

People who are chaste are also people who can love other human beings as they love themselves. They are people who can imagine what it might be like to have a loving relationship destroyed through another person's intervention. They are men and women who are considerate of other people's needs, and who can see that other people's needs might be more important than their own. They are people who are capable of selflessness in their sexual relationships.

Selflessness

Selflessness is not necessarily a virtue. Human beings who always insist on denying themselves, who always put themselves last and who never consider their own needs can be very difficult and unpleasant people to live with, especially if they are aware of their selflessness.

Creative selflessness is a very different quality. It is a quality which brings people into community. It enables them to reach out to other people and to form relationships where giving and receiving are spontaneous expressions of love.

People who are selfless in their sexual relationships are men and women who give themselves to other people in relationships which are based on love. They are concerned to give pleasure to those to whom they relate, and to enjoy pleasure themselves, but they realize that real love transcends any self-centred need for sexual gratification because freely given love finds its fulfilment in other people's happiness and growth. People who know the meaning of selfless love are, therefore, able to give up the personal satisfaction of sexual gratification, and even their own happiness, if they think that their sacrifice will enable the person whom they love to become a more whole and truly fulfilled person. The same kind of selfless love can inspire people to put the needs of a group or community of people ahead of their own needs as individuals.

This kind of love is at its zenith when it is unself-conscious, yet visible to others. Such selfless love undoubtedly enables some men and women to break off their relations with those whom they love deeply, but who are already committed to other relationships and responsibilities. Such heroic self-sacrifice sometimes amounts to their 'laying down their lives for their friends', and it commands admiration from their counsellors and friends who know the cost of such self-sacrifice. In less obvious but no less real ways people who live together as sexual partners or in religious communities are constantly making sacrifices for each other because of their mutual love.

Selflessness is a virtue which cannot be taught to clients by counsellors. Like chastity, selflessness is the consequence of love, and many clients who come to counsellors with sexual problems have only slender experiences of friendship and love upon which they can build new and unselfish loving relationships. Yet the counselling relationship, if it is also a friendship, can provide clients with some valuable opportunities of learning to recognize and appreciate sacrificial love.

Sacrificial love and selfless love may involve giving up a relationship for the sake of other people, but it may also prompt people to be faithful to committed relationships.

Fidelity

Fidelity is a virtue which enables people to persevere with their relationships. It is a prized quality in sexual partnerships of all kinds. When, for instance, two people plan to set up home together they usually want to pledge themselves to each other, irrespective of their religious belief, and the spoken or unspoken vows and promises they make to each other are generally made whole-heartedly with the intention of staying together on a permanent basis.

Marriage and friendship vows are, like religious vows, usually interpreted strictly as regards physical fidelity. Nuns and monks, for instance, take vows of chastity for the love of God, and this means that they promise not

167

to have sexual intercourse. Celibate clergy promise to remain single in the same way. Married people promise to be faithful to each other for the duration of their lives, and this usually means that they promise not to have physical relations outside the marriage. Similarly, sometimes the partners to a gay union make a contract to remain physically faithful to each other.

Physical fidelity is usually seen to be the sign of a deeper commitment to a continuing relationship of love. Many people, therefore, feel that if the physical part of the promise is violated then the whole relationship is threatened. Such a strict attitude towards vows of fidelity can have serious consequences. Celibate priests have, for instance, been known to leave the priesthood because they have committed fornication on one occasion. Wives have divorced their husbands after the first incident of adultery. Gay friends have separated after a single act of physical infidelity.

When so much emphasis is placed on physical fidelity that a deeper relationship is seriously threatened when the physical vow is broken even once, it must affect people's attitudes towards the relationships to which they are vowed. Total fidelity of an all-or-nothing kind tends to force the people concerned into a closed relationship in which the couple 'keep themselves to themselves' and so gradually lose their friends and outside interests.

Such a view of fidelity is certainly present in some people's minds, and unfaithfulness to it causes much distress on occasion. Some women, for instance, find themselves tormented by jealousy when their husbands prefer to go out in the evenings with other men friends instead of staying at home with their families. They can be equally unhappy if their ambitious husbands put a lot of their time and energy into their chosen profession. Husbands can be equally jealous if their wives get too deeply involved with their careers or with their children. Fear of this kind of unfaithfulness can lead a couple to

168

lock themselves into a relationship from which everyone else and all outside interests are excluded.

Creative fidelity does not result in this kind of 'shut-in' relationship. A commitment to creative fidelity might inspire people to make vows of chastity or physical fidelity but it will also enable them to live in 'open' relationships which can include other people rather than having to keep them out. In such a marriage, for instance, each partner will set the other free to make friendships outside the home. The same can be true of the partners of a gay union or of celibate communities.

Creative fidelity thrives on the partners' outside interests and friendships of all kinds. It enables individuals to bring into their families a wealth of experience from outside their homes. This experience can enrich the lives of other members of the unit and enable it to grow in new directions.

People who are committed to each other in this kind of faithful relationship where they share a joint home and family unit are likely to be able to survive considerable stresses in their intimate relationships. The occasional act of physical infidelity does not necessarily threaten the stability of such a union.

There is some evidence to suggest that until recently men who married did not see their own marital infidelities as threatening to the marriage. On the other hand they did not tolerate unfaithfulness in their wives at all well. Women, on the whole, seemed to adopt a more rigid attitude towards faithfulness in marriage because of their relative seclusion in the home on account of the children, and their consequent emotional dependence on the one man with whom they come into frequent and intimate contact. Certainly it would be true to say that until the last two decades women and men adopted a double standard of morality as regards sexual behaviour. Thirty years ago it was generally accepted that men could 'sow their wild oats' before marriage and commit adultery after marriage without necessarily harming themselves and their families. Women were considered to damage themselves if they 'slept around' with men before marriage, or if they dared to be unfaithful after marriage. These attitudes have now changed in most sections of the western community. The social relationships between women and men have greatly changed during the past twenty to twenty-five years. It is now far more common than it was to meet women as well as men with more liberal attitudes towards extra-marital friendships and extra-marital sexual intercourse. Consequently, many more people are having to face the consequences of those liberal attitudes in their own lives.

If this new single standard of morality for men and women alike is to gain ground then it will be necessary for the relationship between the sexes to alter radically. Those who want to claim their freedom within the marital relationship so far as physical, sexual intercourse goes, but who wish to commit themselves to a stable and permanent relationship, will have to base their partnership on different foundations. They will need to make open contracts with each other at the beginning of their relationship, and they will need to review those contracts at regular intervals. The people who are committed to each other in a particular relationship are the only ones who can decide whether or not they can face the kind of emotional upheavals which might occur if one or both of them engaged in sexual intercourse with people outside their own partnership. Some liberally minded people have been unpleasantly surprised to discover the strength of their negative reactions to a partner's extra-marital infidelities. However, it does seem possible that physical infidelity can be consistent with a concept of permanent fidelity to a relationship, provided that both partners accept a kind of contract different from a vow of physical fidelity upon which to base their relational faithfulness.

In this sensitive area of relationships it is interesting

to note that all kinds of variation on the familiar dyadic union can and do exist. Many of them indicate that the individuals concerned have adapted themselves to a situation which many other people would have found intolerable. One family doctor, for instance, cared for a happily married couple with three children where the wife had a lesbian relationship with a friend. This extra-marital relationship was so acceptable to the husband that he invited his wife's friend to stay in their house with them. Neither he nor his wife thought of her relationship as adulterous, although both of them agreed that the situation would have been intolerable if she had taken a male lover. In another general practice the doctor looked after two groups of three people where one woman was living with two men. In one family the woman had two lovers: in the other the men were the lovers. In yet another group all three people were lovers. Every family doctor will know a number of women who are able to tolerate the adultery of their husbands without recrimination.

These triadic and multiple relationships are not necessarily creative just because they are tolerated. The dynamics of such partnerships can be very destructive, for instance, when two people collude with each other to exclude, isolate or hurt the third member of the triad. It does, however, appear to be true that some couples have learnt that there is no way by which each partner can fully satisfy the other's needs, and one or both of them have then released the other partner to find fulfilment through another person who can supply the missing quality. Sometimes both partners are able to take lovers by mutual consent.

Counsellors are bound to come into contact with an increasing number of people who are living together in these kinds of unusual way because the western tradition of monogamy has apparently failed them, or they have failed to conform to its demands. Some of these irregular unions are successful at a pragmatic level, and it is impossible to condemn them out of hand. Counsellors who are convinced of the wisdom of the traditional relationships which are based on the Christian ethic will have to take these new modes of relationship seriously as they will undoubtedly meet increasing numbers of families and family groups where monogamy is no longer mandatory, and where an appeal to return to Christian monogamous patterns of relationship will fall on deaf ears.

The attack on the Christian ethic is not only coming from those who cannot, or do not want to, live according to its ideals even though they have been brought up in countries which are influenced by Christian ideals. In addition, as more contacts are established between western and Third-World countries, the western-style institution of monogamous marriage will be challenged by some of the stable unions which can be found in polygamous and polyandrous societies. It is too early to say what effect the mingling of cultures taking place all over the world will have on the western pattern of dyadic marriage. If alternative patterns of close family relationship are seen to be conducive to the happiness and welfare of the whole family, then monogamous marriage, as practised in all western societies, will have to be re-examined as the only legal union which is presently permitted in western countries.

At present in the West life-long monogamous unions coexist with patterns of divorce and remarriage which can be described as legalized serial monogamy. Gay unions exist but have no legal validity. Polygamy and polyandry are practised, especially among immigrant peoples, but they are illegal. There is an impression that, with the decline of Christianity in the West and the mingling of cultures, polygamy and polyandry command more acceptance among the indigenous peoples of western countries than is evident from public statements by 'top' people. Nuclear marriage is certainly under attack, and the search for new-style family living has moved from the academics to the communes where people are trying to test out their beliefs in practice.

Some writers have observed the rapidly changing social trends in western society and have seen the impact which the women's movement has made on the relations between men and women. As long ago as 1972, for instance, a feminist writer, Daphne Nash, wrote:

One of the social and economic structures which is in the early stages of such change is the nuclear family, for such reasons as those outlined above. Alternative forms of community will become established where children will be brought up with attitudes to community and human relationships more and more different from the present ones as time goes on and new structures emerge. The Liverpool Free School is one such move in the right direction. What constitutes the most important inter-personal relationship for a community's continued progress will in all probability admit of much more variation than at present. In a community without private property, where children are raised in common or by those who want to and are good at it (have a 'vocation'), there will not be the need there has been hitherto for one person to be the 'head' or paterfamilias, and it is for instance possible that the basic unit of a community would be the commune (perhaps half a dozen or more adults plus children). In this case the Church would have to rethink the theology of marriage; it would seem counter-creative in such a case not to allow the sacramental validity of the unconditional commitment of several adults to one another. The Church has existed through several stages of the economic and political advance of history—slave-owning antiquity, feudalism and capitalism. Bound up as it is with the concept of private property, monogamy in one form or another has been the only absolutely necessary form of marriage so far. As the relations of property ownership change, monogamy may be recognized as only one form among others of the creative inter-personal commitment necessary for the well-being of society.[4]

In the following year another Christian writer, Fr Adrian Hastings, was reporting on his experience in Africa. He put forward his views in the same journal:

In a seriously polygamous society I would expect the Christian gospel preached with a clear intimation of a Christian's future commitment to monogamous marriage to make slow progress, but there is no great harm in that, anyway: the Church's significance derives from the sacramental quality of the living of a minority, not from mass baptisms. However, even in extensively polygamous societies the majority of adult males are not and cannot be polygamous, the balance of the sexes dictates this, so the existence of a religious minority committed to monogamy is in no way socially impossible. Whereas, however, the traditional majority would hold to a marital ideal of polygamy, the Christian minority would hold to one of monogamy; in so doing—as in many other ways too—it creates a counter-culture. This is perfectly healthy. Cultures do not need to be monolithic; where they are, they tend to be oppressive. Where they exist in any extensive form they necessarily include within them counter-cultures of one kind and another. That Christian belief results in such a thing wherever it is sincerely received is only to be expected.[5]

These two writers have been extensively quoted because they show so well that the concept of fidelity, as hitherto understood and accepted in western society, is under pressure. Since they wrote their articles the stability of many more families has been threatened by the rising number of divorces, and failed communes, and so people of every persuasion are actively searching for creative solutions to the problems which have been raised by the breakdown of family stability. Some of these creative solutions may come through a restatement of the Christian ethic of strict monogamy: others may come through a reinterpretation of the concept of fidelity and its relationship to the stability of a family as a suitable environment for the nurture of children. The latter approach would seem to command the support of the greatest number of people, although Christians would feel, on the whole, that physical faithfulness was an important factor in preserving the concept of fidelity, as a stabilizing factor in the family and community. Their continued witness to their beliefs are thought to be an important and valuable contribution to a changing society.

Sexual counselling is a practical art. Counsellors and therapists relate to a variety of people in different kinds of partnership. Many of these people have disturbed relationships. They find it difficult to believe that it is possible for them to enjoy any enduring relationship based on friendship, loyalty and faithfulness. Counsellors can provide such an ongoing relationship for some of their clients.

It is a fact of life that some friendships and many professional counselling relationships last for longer than some marriages and sexual partnerships. Clients who are fortunate enough to enjoy such long-standing associations can draw on the full benefit of a friend's or counsellor's knowledge of their characters when they are most in need of help. They, in turn, can give their counsellors the sort of loyalty that encourages counsellors to feel that their work is worth while, even sometimes that they are loved for what they are rather than for what they do for their clients.

Love

A book on sexual counselling would be incomplete without any mention of love since most clients are more concerned with problems about love than with problems about sex. Yet, it is almost impossible to define love without resorting to clichés, and it is certainly impossible to teach anyone a technique of loving in the same way as one is able to teach someone to cope with a sexual problem. In connection with sexual counselling it seems best to describe love as romance and reality tucked up together in the same bed, and to leave people free to work out the implications of love for themselves in their own special situations.

Words are inadequate to describe that surge of desire towards another which is called love, and it is easier for clients and counsellors to keep to the pedestrian paths and talk about sexuality instead of trying to scale the heights

of human experience. Yet from time to time it is essential
that either in words or in silence counsellors and clients
should allow themselves to look beyond the reason for their
work together towards the ultimate goal of the experience
of love. That experience cannot be captured by any one
person for all people, but something of its essence is caught
in the poem which ends this book, and which was written
by a nun-poet in the solitude of silence.

> The thing called love
> Yes, I have experienced it now,
> The thing called love.
> Not in consuming passion of desire, but in near-far fire:
> Not in the voice, but in the ear.
> It is a steeling of the heart to bear
> The pain where I in sympathy depart to share
> Another's sphere.
> Where all I thought I cared about, I lose
> Without care.
> Eager to be where only my love is
> And find Him there.[6]

APPENDIX A
Definitions of Counselling

COUNSELLING

The giving of advice on personal, social, psychological etc. problems as an occupation (Supplement *O.E.D.*, 1972).

A dialogue in which one person helps another who has some difficulty that is important to him (J. H. Wallis. *Personal Counselling*, Allen and Unwin 1973).

A process designed to help a person answer the question 'What shall I do?' (Leona Tyler. *The Work of the Counsellor*, Appleton-Century Crofts 1961).

An enabling process, designed to help an individual to come to terms with his life as it is and ultimately to grow to greater maturity through learning to take responsibility and to make decisions himself (Anne Jones. *School Counselling in Practice*, Ward Lock 1970).

Counselling is the way in which a counsellor and his client relate to each other in the exploration together of the client's problem and possible solutions to it. Counselling is generally differentiated from the treatment of patients; its basic orientation is not to psychopathology but to the types of problem people encounter at different stages of their normal human development (A. J. M. Thompson. *An Investigation into the Work Performed by Some Trained Counsellors in English Secondary Schools*, University of Keele 1970).

APPENDIX B

On the Formulation of Criteria for Distinguishing between Creative and Destructive Patterns of Sexual Behaviour

The distinction between creative and destructive sexual behaviour can be made only by personal judgement. This judgement must depend upon the counsellor's personal value-system and her or his personal experience of its limitations and assets.

As a counsellor I have found it impossible to assess all sexual behaviour against an absolute standard of right and wrong which can be applied to every person and situation in all circumstances. I have also found it impossible to work with people without making any value-judgements at all other than adopting the client's own value-systems. The situational ethicist's desire to use Love as the standard against which to measure all behaviour has been very attractive to me. In practice the concept of love has proved itself liable to so many differences of interpretation that I have found myself obliged to try to define it more precisely.

As a Christian I believe that the perfection of God who is Love is to be found in the Trinity. The persons of the Trinity, often named as Father, Son and Holy Spirit, have distinctive functions which express different aspects of Love at work throughout creation. These distinctive functions are conveyed in the alternative names of the persons of the Trinity. God can be described equally well as God, Creator, Redeemer and Sustainer, and those names convey the distinctive functions of the different persons within the unity of the Trinity. Hence it becomes possible to define the work of Love more precisely in terms of creativity, reconciliation and growth and to affirm that God, the blessed Trinity, is actively present wherever there are signs of creativity, reconciliation and growth in individuals or communities, or, indeed, in creation itself.

Since Christians believe that men and women are made 'in

the image of God' it is to be expected that they will be most 'like' that image when they are engaged in work which can be described as creative in that it results in the production of new life, harmony and growth. This analogy between the Trinity and men and women who are the flower of God's creation is easy to understand if we look at how human beings share in God's work when they come together to procreate children.

Although it is only a rough comparison there is a sense in which it is possible to say that as God is the creator of life so people become 'like' God when they conceive new life. As Christ is the one who brings all things into harmony with the Creator, so women and men are 'like' Christ when they are united with each other and their union is blessed with children. As the Holy Spirit is the breath of God, the giver of life who sustains and strengthens people, so they are 'like' the Holy Spirit when they strengthen and sustain each other and their children.

It is comparatively easy to see how men and women can be described as being 'like' God when they co-operate with God in the mystery of procreation. That is not, however, the only way in which they share in God's creativity. Procreativity does not necessarily confine itself to the birth of new biological life. God is fecund in all sorts of other ways, and women and men who never have children are as able to share in God's fecundity as those people who produce new human beings to carry on the human race.

If we accept that God is always at work within creation, ceaselessly active to bring new life into being, to reconcile all creation to its source, to enable it to grow towards its ultimate destiny, then we should be able to use the Trinity as a basis for recognizing this divine activity at work in all creation and especially in the affairs of women and men. We have already seen that human beings can be said to be 'like' God when they conceive and bear and rear children in Love. We can extend that analogy to include all kinds of other human activities which are creative.

In practice I have found it helpful to use this model of the Trinity as a guide-line to help me to decide which course of action is most creative, most 'like' God. For instance, before making a close relationship with anyone it may be necessary to ask for people to question themselves about the potential of the relationship. Will it result in new life, or not? Will it bring about a greater harmony between the individuals concerned and also deepen their unity with all the other people who are likely to be affected by the new relationship or activity? Will it promote the growth of the people involved and the communities in which they live? These kinds of question can also be asked about existing relationships. The guide-lines are particularly useful when everything seems to be going wrong and the people concerned are having to decide whether to go on with the relationship on a new basis or break it off.

In the course of my own work I have tried to look at various sexual activities and at people's problems, including my own, against these three guide-lines, based on the model of the Trinity. The guide-lines have been effective in helping me to sort out right from wrong in the issues which confront me as a woman and as a doctor. If the relationship is shown to be 'like' God in that it creates new life, brings about unity and harmony and results in new growth then the relationship can be given a 'go-ahead green light'. Once the relationship is established it needs reviewing periodically by the same standards and so long as these three 'marks' of the Trinity are there the green light still shines. But there may come a time when there are warning signs in evidence which suggest that all is not well and that the three signs of wholeness are partially or wholly obscured by sterility, disunity and the death of relationships between individuals and whole families, and/or communities in society.

When these warning signs are present then people have to think very seriously about the new or established relationship or activity in which they have become involved. The red 'stop-light' does not necessarily mean that the relationship must come to a permanent end. It merely warns people that they need to review their behaviour and the basis of the relations as a whole if they want to keep the relationship alive. If they ignore the red light they do so on their own responsibility and if they persist in going ahead when there are clear signs to stop then either they or other people will inevitably suffer. They may kill a precious friendship or working relationship and destroy a work of God. If, however, they do recognize the authority of the warning signs they may be able to 'turn back' or 'alter direction' in such a way that they and those whom they love are willing to sacrifice their immediate joy in each other for the sake of ultimate fulfilment.

Guide-lines cannot be rigid laws. They do not absolve anyone from making responsible judgements. They are not the only criteria for making important decisions in one's life and they may not be useful to anyone other than myself. They have, however, stood the test of many years' medical practice and they have certainly proved to be helpful in defining which relationships are likely to survive a crisis and which can be severed because the relationship is already moribund or dead.

APPENDIX C
Useful Books and Contacts

Every counsellor builds up a useful personal list of books and contacts with healing agencies. The following lists contain only books and agencies well known to me which I have found outstandingly helpful.

ONE: Sex and Self

Exploring Sex Differences, B. Lloyd and J. Archer. Academic Press 1976.
Conundrum, J. Morris. Faber & Faber 1974.
A Gender Trap Pt 2. Sex, Love and Marriage, C. Adams. Virago 1976.
Our Bodies, Ourselves, Boston Woman's Health Collective. Simon & Schuster 1976; Penguin 1979.
Contemporary Schools of Psychology, R. S. Woodward, Methuen 1965.
Psychoanalysis and Women, ed. J. Miller. Penguin 1973.

TWO: Sexual Relationships

The Joy of Sex, Alex Comfort. Quartet Books 1974.
The Book of Love, D. Delvin. New English Library 1975.
Sex and Life, B. Ward. McDonald Guidelines 1978.
The Family and Marriage in Britain, R. Fletcher. Penguin 1973.
Homosexuality from the Inside, D. Blamires. Social Responsibility Council of the Religious Society of Friends 1977.

THREE: Some Moral Problems

Psychology of Moral Behaviour, D. Wright. Penguin 1971.
Marital Breakdown, J. Dominian. Penguin 1972.
The Church and the Homosexual, J. J. McNeil. Darton, Longman & Todd 1977.

Towards a Theology of Gay Liberation, M. Macourt. S.C.M. 1977.

Moral Questions, F. Colquoun. C.P.A.S. 1977.

Sex and Christian Freedom, L. Hodgson. S.C.M. 1967.

Proposals for a New Sexual Ethic, J. Dominian. Darton, Longman & Todd 1977.

FOUR: Destructive Sex

Basic Sexual Medicine, E. Trimmer. Heinemann Medical 1978.

Against Our Will, S. Brownmiller. Penguin 1977.

Scream Quietly or the Neighbours will Hear, E. Pizzey Penguin 1974.

The following organizations offer help in this field:

    N.S.P.C.C., 1 Riding House Street, London W1

    S.P.U.C., 9a Brechin Place, London SW7

    LIFE, 35 Kenilworth Road, Leamington Spa, Warwicks.

    F.P.A., 27 Mortimer Street, London W1

    P.A.S., 40 Margaret Street, London W1

    N.M.G.C., Herbert Grey College, Rugby

    Institute of Psychosexual Medicine, 111 Harley Street, London w1

FIVE: Sexual Therapy

An Introduction to Pastoral Counselling, K. Heasman. Constable 1969.

Illustrated Manual of Sex Therapy, H. Kaplan. Souvenir Press 1968 (expensive but worth it).

Sex and Life, B. Ward. McDonald Guidelines 1978 (cheap and good for lending).

Human Sexual Inadequacy, W. H. Masters and V. Johnson. J. A. Churchill Limited (massive book but well worth reading).

Forum Magazine—consistently high standard.

Psychosexual Problems, D. Friedan. (These are three tapes on common problems and treatments, including Balint seminars and Masters and Johnson technique.) Available from Medical Recording Foundation, P.O. Box 99, Chelmsford, CM1 5HZ.

Sex Aids (These are available from R. Price who runs a shop called Phyllis Wright Limited, 34 St George's Walk, Croydon CR0 1YJ.)

The following agencies are always helpful:

Westminster Pastoral Foundation, Maria Assumpta College, Kensington, London W8

Family Planning Association, 27 Mortimer Street, London W1 (they train counsellors in psychosexual skills).

Institute of Psychosexual medicine, 111 Harley Street, London W1

National Marriage Guidance Council, Herbert Grey College, Rugby

Clinical Theology Association, Mount Hooton Road, Nottingham.

Samaritans, See local Telephone Directories for nearest branch.

SIX: Creative Sex

The Holy Bible is the only book to which I constantly refer.

Notes

Introduction

1 Dualism: (a) A philosophical doctrine which holds that mind and matter are distinct, equally real, and not essentially related, as opposed to monism, which asserts that all that exists has a single ultimate nature.

   (b) A metaphysical system which holds that good and evil are the outcome or product of separate and equally ultimate first causes. (*Oxford Dictionary of the Christian Church*)

2 The Gnostics made a distinction between the supreme Divine Being and the Demiurge or 'creator god', a lesser being who was the immediate source of creation and ruled the world. As the Demiurge was a 'fallen being' so the world was imperfect and antagonistic to what was truly spiritual.

3 The Christian doctrine of the Incarnation holds to the view that the historical Christ is at once fully God and fully man without the integrity of either being impaired. Since the eternal Son of God put on human flesh, matter is seen as a fit vehicle for the divine.

ONE: Sex and Self

1 Morris J., *Conundrum* (Faber & Faber 1974), p. 9.

2 Erickson E., *Childhood and Society* (W. W. Norton & Co. Inc., N.Y. 1950). Quoted in Essay by D. Ullian: *Exploring Sex Differences*. B. Lloyd and J. Archer (Academic Press 1976), p. 27.

3 Seidenberg R., 'Is Anatomy Destiny?' Quoted in *Psycho-analysis and Women*, ed. J. B. Miller (Penguin 1974), p. 325.

4 King J. S., *Women and Work*. D.E.M.P. (H.M.S.O. 1974), p. 17.

5 Lloyd B. and Archer J., *Exploring Sex Differences* (Academic Press 1976), p. 177.

6 ibid., p. 178.

7 King J. S., *Women and Work*. D.E.M.P. (H.M.S.O. 1974), p. 31.

8 Ullian D. S., 'Development of Gender Concepts', *Exploring Sex Differences*, B. Lloyd and J. Archer (Academic Press 1976), p. 25.

9 ibid., p. 44.

10 ibid., p. 44.

11 Messent., 'Female Hormones and Behaviour', *Exploring Sex Differences* (Academic Press 1976), p. 190.

TWO: Sexual Relationships

1   Smith J. A. K., *Free Fall* (S.P.C.K. 1977), p. 77.
2   Hite S., *The Hite Report* (Dell Publishing Co. Inc., N.Y. 1977). Ms Hite does not deal with fantasy as a separate subject but her section on masturbation (pp. 59–120) reveals the importance of fantasy in the sexual arousal of many women.
3   Dominian J., *Proposals for a New Sexual Ethic* (Darton, Longman & Todd 1977), p. 26.
4   Masters and Johnson, *Human Sexual Inadequacy* (Little, Brown and Co. 1970), p. 26.

THREE: Some Moral Problems

1   In this context an absolutist is a person who believes that there are values which maintain their validity under any and every circumstance, no matter what.
2   *Penguin Dictionary of Psychology*, ed. J. Drever 1952, p. 88.
3   Wilde O., *Picture of Dorian Gray*, Penguin 1949.
4   Caswell J. R., *The Dying Patient*, ed. R. W. Raven (Pitman Medical 1975), p. 118.

FOUR: Destructive Sex

1   Storr A., *The Dynamics of Creation* (Penguin 1976), p. 169.
2   ibid., pp. 169–70.
3   Bronmiller S., *Against Our Will* (Martin, Secker & Warburg 1975; Penguin Books 1977), p. 15.
4   Pizzey E., *Scream Quietly or the Neighbours Will Hear* (Penguin 1974).
5   The writer considers that there is an important difference between casual sexual relationships and promiscuous ones even though they are treated together in the text. People may resort to casual sex for a variety of reasons including loneliness, hunger and fear, but those who are promiscuous are habitually greedy and undiscriminating in their selection of partners.
6   Agencies like the Josephine Butler Society and the Church Army have made detailed studies on prostitution and can be consulted on this complex question. A useful article on 'Prostitution in the Inner City' may be found in *Crucible*, Peter Chapman (C.I.O. 1976), p. 18.
7   Stafford Clark D., *What Freud Really Said* (Penguin 1967).

8 There are numerous books on this subject. One of the best introductions remains the classic study by R. S. Woodworth: *Contemporary Schools of Psychology*, revised in collaboration with Professor Mary Sheridan in 1964 and published in Britain in 1965 by Methuen.

9 Most abortions are carried out by vacuum aspiration or curettage in very early stages of pregnancy (under 12 weeks' gestation), by curettage between 12 and 16 weeks and by abdominal operation (hysterotomy) after 16 weeks. All foetuses, everywhere, are considered to be capable of independent existence after 28 weeks of gestation. Some babies can and do live when they are born 2–4 weeks earlier than this. For this reason many doctors support moves to reduce the upper time limit for legal abortion to 24 or 20 weeks' gestation.

10 Reversal operations can be carried out for both women and men. Their success cannot be guaranteed. The overall success rate is only about 50 per cent at the present time.

11 Modern techniques of laparoscopic sterilization have reduced the risks to women. Operative techniques are improving rapidly and in expert hands this method is now as effective as the more conventional operation which involves open access through an abdominal incision to allow the fallopian tubes to be divided and tied.

FIVE: Sexual Therapy

1 Jones A., *School Counselling in Practice* (Ward Lock 1970), p. 10.
2 Skynner R., *One Flesh, Two Separate Persons* (Constable 1976), p. 74.
3 Fletcher J., *Situation Ethics* (S.C.M. Press Ltd 1966), p. 33.
4 ibid., p. 33.
5 ibid., p. 154.
6 Skynner R., *One Flesh, Two Separate Persons* (Constable 1976), p. 79.
7 Master and Johnson, *Human Sexual Inadequacy* (Little, Brown and Co. 1970), p. 389.
8 There are a great many other forms of treatment like hypnotherapy, Gestalt therapy, encounter therapy, co-counselling, primal-scream therapy. Most of these can be useful to people with particular needs. They are usually available from specialists or at special centres but are not so useful to the generalists for whom this book is intended. That is why they do not find a place in the main text.

SIX: Creative Sex

1 Evening M., *Who Walk Alone* (Hodder & Stoughton 1974), p. 220.
2 Russel G., *Women and Men* (S.C.M. 1973) p. 77.
3 Goergen D., *The Sexual Celibate* (S.P.C.K. 1976), p. 103.
4 Nash D., 'Women's Liberation and Christian Marriage' (*New Blackfriars* May 1972), p. 20.
5 Hastings A., 'A Report on Marriage' (*New Blackfriars*, June 1973), pp. 257–8.
6 Sr Agnes Mary, *Daffodils in Ice*. (Workshop Press 1972).

Index